# Memories
## of
# Edinburgh

*Part of the*
## Memories
*series*

*The Publishers would like to thank the following companies for
supporting the production of this book*

Dominion Cinemas

The Edinburgh Academy

George Hardie & Son (Joiners) Limited

William Hunter Coaches (Loanhead) Limited

Kwik-Fit Holdings plc

John G Mackintosh Electrical Engineers & Contractors

R&J Malone's Bakeries

Merchiston Castle School

Mr Boni's Ice Cream

SCA Packaging Limited

Scobie & McIntosh (Bakery Engineers) Limited

William E Scott & Son

Whytock & Reid

First published in Great Britain by True North Books Limited
Units 3 - 5 Heathfield Industrial Park
Elland West Yorkshire
HX5 9AE
Tel. 01422 377977
© Copyright: True North Books Limited 1999

ISBN 1 900463 33 4

*Text, design and origination by True North Books Limited, Elland, West Yorkshire
Printed and bound by The Amadeus Press Limited, Huddersfield, West Yorkshire*

# Memories are made of this

**M**emories. We all have them; some good, some bad, but our memories of the city we grew up in are usually tucked away in a very special place in our minds. The best are usually connected with our childhood and youth, when we longed to be grown up and paid no attention to adults who told us to enjoy being young, as these were the best years of our lives. We look back now and realise that they were right.

So many memories - perhaps of the war and rationing, perhaps of Festivals, parades, celebrations and Royal visits. And so many changes; the outdoor swimming pool at Portobello that came and went, one-way traffic systems and pedestrianisation. New trends in shopping led to the very first self-serve stores being opened - and the self-service restaurant in Jenners came as a bit of a culture shock at first to many of the famous store's customers!

Through the bad times and the good, however, Edinburgh not only survived but prospered. We have only to look at the city as it is today, with its finest buildings now cleaned and restored to their full glory, and the traditional tourist attractions now complemented by up-to-the-minute facilities, to see what progress has been realised and what achievements have been made over the last 50 years. Edinburgh has a history to be proud of - but more importantly, a great future to look forward to, into the new millennium and beyond.

# Contents

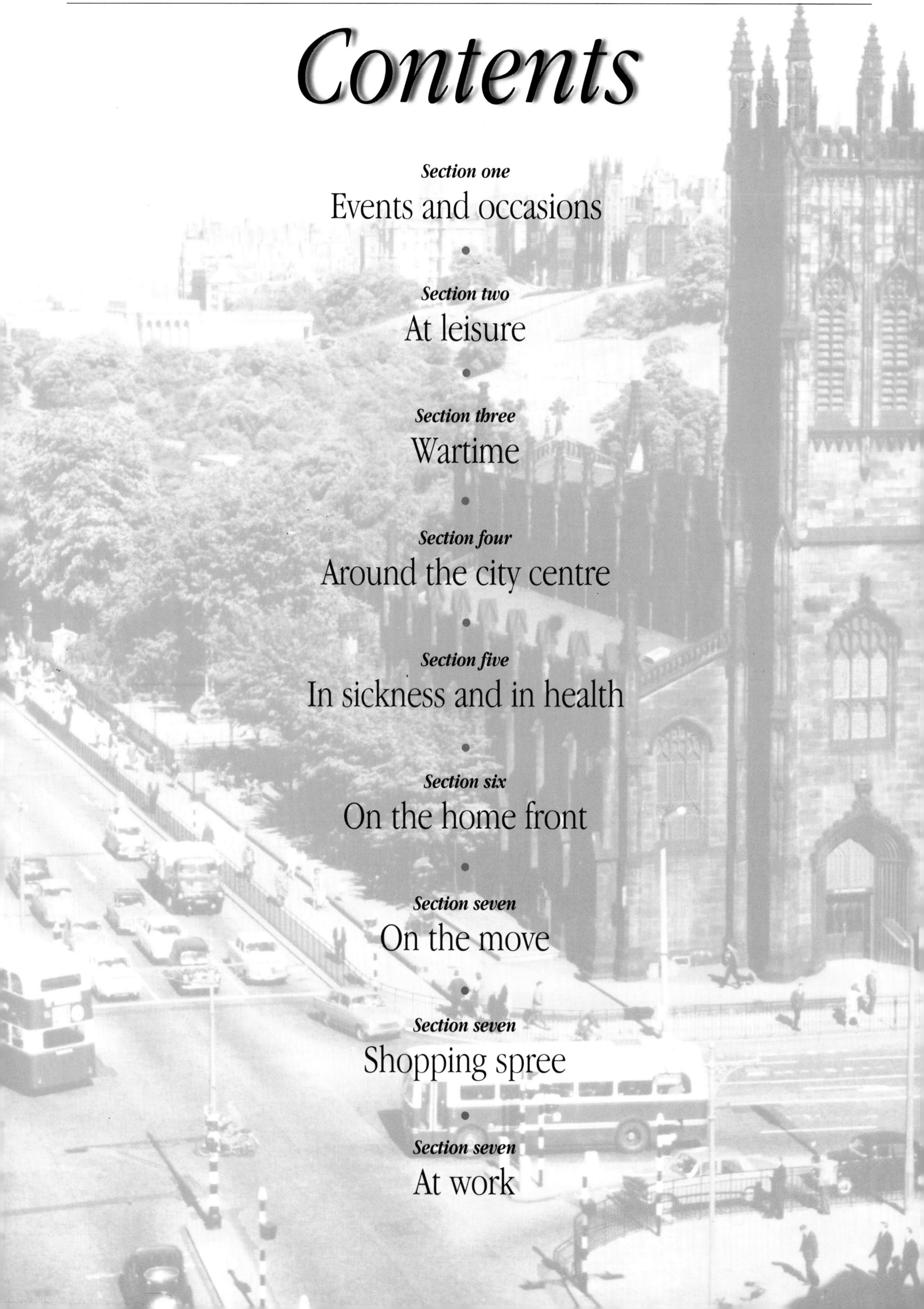

*Section one*

Events and occasions

•

*Section two*

At leisure

•

*Section three*

Wartime

•

*Section four*

Around the city centre

•

*Section five*

In sickness and in health

•

*Section six*

On the home front

•

*Section seven*

On the move

•

*Section seven*

Shopping spree

•

*Section seven*

At work

# Events & occasions

In 1927, in the Fishermen's Hall in Newhaven, the audience awaiting an address by the prospective MP for Leith, Ernest Brown, became restless at his unpunctuality. A Mrs Ritchie organised some singing to fill the time, and on his arrival Mr Brown was so enchanted by the sound, that he declared that the singers ought to form a proper choir. This was the birth of the Newhaven Fisherwomen's Choir which, under the leadership of Mrs Ritchie, went from strength to strength and had performed three times in London by 1939.

The Choir was invited to sing at the Fisheries Exhibition at Trondheim, Norway, and the photograph shows a section of the Choir just prior to departure, in 1965. The Ritchie family involvement was still strong, and the two ladies in ordinary dress are her daughters - `Menie' or Marion, to the left, being the conductor, and Betty, to the right, being the pianist. The choristers are dressed in the traditional festive attire of Newhaven fishwives, a design of red-and-white and yellow-and-white stripes, a short gown and a Paisley shawl.

On a memorable trip, the Choir gave five concerts, one of which was attended by King Olaf and his family.

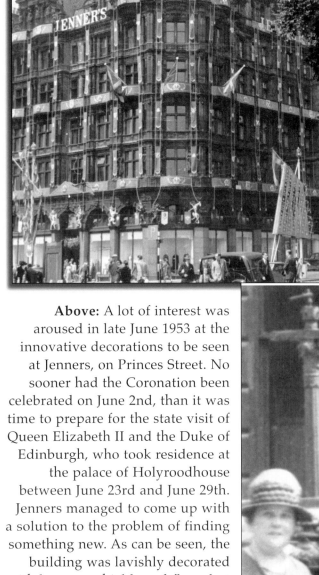

**Above:** A lot of interest was aroused in late June 1953 at the innovative decorations to be seen at Jenners, on Princes Street. No sooner had the Coronation been celebrated on June 2nd, than it was time to prepare for the state visit of Queen Elizabeth II and the Duke of Edinburgh, who took residence at the palace of Holyroodhouse between June 23rd and June 29th. Jenners managed to come up with a solution to the problem of finding something new. As can be seen, the building was lavishly decorated with banners, shields and flags, but what caught the public's eye was the series of replicas of the `Queen's Beasts' between the upper parts of the ground floor windows. Lions, griffins and unicorns were featured, amongst others, emblazoned in full heraldic colour. Between each pair of beasts there were royal coats-of-arms. Huge, cheering crowds greeted the Queen and Prince Philip on June 23rd as they progressed through the streets of Edinburgh in a horse-drawn open carriage. This was the beginning of a busy week for the royal couple, perhaps one of the highlights being their attendance at `The Masque of Edinburgh' historical pageant at Usher Hall, on June 27th.

Pageant Day for the Co-operative Children's Circle sees everyone turned out in their very best. Ankle and knee socks positively gleam white and there is a wonderful array of 1920s hats on show. One boy and his dog look down from a float which seems to be extolling the merits of CWS tea. It is difficult now to appreciate the impact that was once made on people's lives by the Co-operative Movement. Edinburgh used to have three retail co-operative societies - St Cuthbert's, Leith Provident, and Portobello - backed by their own Wholesale Association, complete with flour mills. In 1923 St Cuthbert's had the highest turnover of any co-op in Britain, and by 1960 it acted like a retailing version of the Welfare State, providing services `from the cradle to the grave.' The dividend was one of the big attractions to customers, and many older readers will be able to recite their old `store' number instantly. Some profits were always set aside for educational purposes. Education Committees would finance pageants such as the one pictured, but would also put on courses covering such activities as first aid, choral singing, country dancing, elocution and drama. Finance was also provided for youth groups in the city's suburbs.

**Above:** As an old fishing port, founded around 1500, Newhaven has a rich history that is intertwined with the sea. Local pageants have always reflected this, and although the tradition has not been unbroken, this picture of the 1955 pageant is a reminder of the link between Newhaven and its sea-going past. The boat `Gratitude' noses its way across from Granton Harbour, to the sound of a piper, whilst the Pageant Queen, Maureen Linton, sits in state surrounded by her attendants. These were all pupils of the Victoria School, which has always been conscious of Newhaven's history and maintains a small museum. Older residents will probably remember the huge and colourful pageants of the inter-war years in support of both Leith Hospital and the Royal Infirmary, which were great social events on the calendar. In its early years, the greatest event in Newhaven, or `Our Lady's Port of Grace' as it was then known, was the building and launching of the `Great Michael,' on behalf of James IV. It was the greatest warship of its day, costing £30,000 to build and practically deforesting Fife of oak for its construction. It was never a success; was sold to France; and left to rot in Brest Harbour.

**Below:** This royal occasion for the people of Newhaven is thought to be a `flying' visit by the newly-crowned George VI, accompanied by Queen Elizabeth, in 1937. With the fishwives in their traditional attire, the residents at the Market Gate are preparing to give a royal welcome. In the 1930s Newhaven had retained its tradition as a close-knit fishing community for over 400 years, the Society of Free Fishermen having been founded in 1572. The famous herring fishing began in 1793, and by 1932 about 800 tons of herring were landed annually at Newhaven, along with an even greater quantity of white fish. The fishwives played a full part - mending nets, carrying their huge wicker creels or baskets, and selling direct to housewives in Edinburgh. Their working outfit was based on a navy blue and white striped design. However, for such an event as the one pictured, the fishwives would wear their `gala' outfits - colourful creations in both red-and-white and yellow-and-white stripes - passed down through families. During the 1937 visit, the Queen was presented with two dolls in `gala' costume. Sadly, nothing is left of the old industry other than a Heritage Museum on the site of the old fish market.

**Below:** Jobs with a single employer that last the whole or the best part of a working-life are increasingly rare now. `Mobility' and `reskilling' are the watchwords. This was not the case before and immediately after the last war. Then there was more stability in the job market and long service was more the `norm'. This applied to Mr John Wilson who is pictured here, in 1958, receiving the best wishes of his colleagues. The occasion was that of his retirement as manager of the Ashley Place Branch of the Leith Provident Co-op, on Newhaven Road. Mr Wilson, with 37 years service, was presented with a bookcase, which does seem to reflect the idea that retirement has something to do with leisure. The `gold watch' idea has always seemed on odd one in that you have less need of it when you have retired! Mr Wilson is

second left on the photograph, shaking hands with the new manager, Mr David Martin. Some of the other people present are, from the left, Joe Third (holding camera), Maisie Gibson, Madge Reid and John Finnie. There are some familiar names on the shelves, but some unfamiliar prices, particularly `Meat Pies 4d' ($1^1/_2$p in modern currency.)

**Bottom:** May Day was made a public holiday relatively recently, but the significance of May 1st as the international labour or socialist day dates back to the late nineteenth century. The tradition of Maypole dancing and May Queens, to celebrate the real beginning of spring, reaches right back into pagan times. In all likelihood, these young people on board the Pentland Young Socialists' truck are intent on combining political idealism with a bit of good, old-fashioned May Day revelry. The youngsters leaning on top of the cab certainly appear to be excited and happy. Not that the causes they supported were not serious ones, as the side of the truck makes clear. Vietnam, Alabama, South Africa and Spain were all burning issues of the 1960s, which gives a rough guide to dating the scene. The red banner of the Communist Party follows on behind the truck, held high by men who are probably political veterans in comparison to the young idealists on the truck. A close examination of their posters shows that they have woven local issues into their general plea for world unity and peace. `More houses' is always a powerful `grassroots' message.

*The Miners' Gala in Edinburgh reflected the strength of the coalmining industry in the area*

The radical Scottish political and industrial tradition is reflected in this mammoth trade union procession winding its way through the streets of Edinburgh. The occasion is a Miners' Gala, and the colourful spectacle of the floats to the rear is augmented by the swirl and sound of a pipe band, just in front of the banner of the Polkemmet Branch. Officials of the National Union of Miners front the parade, these being Bill McLean, Eric Clark and John Hendry. That old political 'warhorse,' Michael Foot, swings along too, with stick in hand. The strength of the Miners' Gala in Edinburgh used to reflect the strength of the coalmining industry in Midlothian. Edinburgh and Leith are believed to have been consuming 200,000 tons of coal annually in 1800, most of it being provided by pits that would now find themselves within the District Council's boundaries - Duddingston, Edmonstone, Loanhead, Newton, Sheriffhall and Woolmet. In the 1950s the National Coal Board sunk a lot of investment into two new pits close to Edinburgh, Bilston Glen and Monktonhall. The industry in general has been decimated since the 1980s, and Bilston Glen was closed in 1989. However, at Monktonhall there was a successful miners' buy-out in 1992.

Queen Elizabeth II and the Duke of Edinburgh pause for an informal chat as 25 Learmonth Terrace receives distinguished visitors. This memorable event came in 1975, when the royal couple visited No 2 (City of Edinburgh) Maritime Headquarters Unit of the Royal Auxiliary Air Force. Squadron Leader Pollington is standing next to the young airwoman whom Prince Philip has engaged in conversation. Her clenched hand shows that she is perhaps, quite naturally, feeling the tension of the occasion a little. Just to the rear of the others is Wing Commander Cook, Officer Commanding No 2 Maritime Headquarters Unit. The latter was created in 1959, from former members of 603 Squadron, which had been disbanded two years previously. The building also acts as headquarters for East Lothians Universities Air Squadron, and as regional headquarters for the Air Cadets and the Combined Cadet Force Schools Liaison Officers. Town Headquarters is the focus for recruiting and training Auxiliaries to support the RAF in Scotland and on overseas operational deployments. Number 25 Learmonth Terrace seems a humble address for a royal visit, but it was the former town house of a wine and whisky merchant. It stands in neo-Georgian splendour, and the photograph gives just a glimpse of its interior grandeur.

# *At leisure*

**Above:** Forever frozen in mid-air by the camera, his diving technique isn't up to much, but the young man certainly has courage as he plunges from the top level of the 10 metre tower at Portobello Outdoor Pool. The first municipal baths in Edinburgh opened at Infirmary Street in 1887, partly in response to the health dangers (and the more obvious risks of drowning) which arose from swimming in such places as the Firth of Forth. The outdoor pool at Portobello, which opened in May 1936, measured 90 by 39 metres; could accommodate 1300 bathers simultaneously; and had a 6000 spectator capacity. Its `state of the art' wave-making equipment had such power that, at the opening ceremony, the Lord Provost and his official party were put to flight as a tidal wave bore down on their shallow end viewing position. Edinburgh's climate is perhaps not really suitable for an outdoor pool, and with the increase in other leisure options after World War II, the pool gradually lost popularity. The photograph, taken in June 1965, certainly shows under-used capacity, and by 1978 the annual turnover of swimmers was little more than that of a pre-war Saturday. Sadly, but perhaps inevitably, the pool closed that year.

**Right:** Two symbols of Scottish patriotism seem to face each other across this photograph, one firmly rooted in the past, the other perhaps looking to the future. The sturdy Scottish thistle on the left looks towards the spires of the Assembly Hall across West Princes Street Gardens. The Assembly Hall already served as a focus of one branch of Scottish life in that the General Assembly of the Church of Scotland met there annually, before it was chosen as the temporary home of the new Scottish Parliament. This view of the Gardens dates from 1959, before the clean-up operations on the Royal Scottish Academy and the National Gallery of Scotland. The fact that their fine lines seem almost camouflaged by the trees shows what an amazing difference this cleaning work has made. Now the buildings gleam almost white against their dark backgrounds. The two buildings, designed by William Playfair between 1822 and 1845, stand on an artificial hill, the Mound. It was created out of two million cart-loads of soil from the New Town excavations, being completed around 1820.

**Bottom:** This may well have been the highlight of their visit as a party of school children cluster around the telescope, high on the ramparts of Edinburgh Castle, in June 1965. The view is a fine one across the roofs of Edinburgh towards the high-rise flats of Leith, with the Forth beyond, and Fife in the far distance. The trouble is, of course, that there is only one telescope and a clutch of youngsters anxious to have a go before teacher drags them away to complete their worksheets. The Castle, magnificently situated on its `plug' of volcanic rock, has always had a host of attractions for eager visitors. No doubt these youngsters listened round-eyed to the story of the 300 witches burned between 1479 and 1722 at Witches' Well; or looked with awe at Mons Meg; or tried to peer into the darkness of the 33 metre deep Castle Well. Many readers will have happy memories of school visits to the Castle, but isn't it strange how the bits that stick are not the snippets of information about the saintly Queen Margaret or Cromwell's siege, but the memories of how `little Alan' nearly fell off the ramparts, or of `little Mary' being sick in the bus?

**Right:** `Beauty lies in the eye of the beholder,' runs the old proverb, and to some the appeal of this 1966 picture might lie in the wildness of Salisbury Crags; to others, the attraction might be the distant Edinburgh skyline; some might simply be fascinated by the `vintage' cars on display. Edinburgh is a truly amazing city in that within its boundaries are areas of rugged wilderness. Not far from the densely packed townscape of sophisticated Edinburgh the volcanic Salisbury Crags dramatically `erupt' from the surrounding Queen's Park. The Crags, rising to the height of 247 metres at the famous Arthur's Seat, provide robust walking terrain, and in 1803 Dorothy Wordsworth described the feeling of wildness and solitude there as akin to being on a Highland mountain. That was, of course, before the rise of the modern tourist industry, and the cars in the picture certainly represent the shape of things to come. Good walking and fine views are still there to be enjoyed on Salisbury Crags, but solitude ... well, if the weather is bad! As for car enthusiasts, the view they might be most enjoying is that of the rear end of the Morris Minor 1000, seemingly in mint condition.

*Ross Fountain was created for the International Exhibition of 1862*

West Princes Street Gardens provide a scene of summer relaxation in August 1966. For some, the whole afternoon lazing in a deckchair might be the prospect. For others, it is probably a matter of snatching a brief hour of fresh air before returning to shop or office. The refreshing nature of Ross Fountain, in the middle, cannot be denied, although some have questioned its artistic merits.

This massive piece of cast iron work was created for the International Exhibition of 1862 by an unknown sculptor and later gifted to the city. Dean Edward Ramsay, a prominent figure in the Church of Scotland, described it as `indecent and disgusting.' Nevertheless, leisure is the keynote of this scene, and the nearby Ross Open Air Theatre is a focus for such summer entertainments as piping and Scottish dancing. It is odd to think that from the mid-fifteenth century to the early nineteenth century this scenario would have been one of Nor' Loch lapping against the steep sides of the Castle rock.

This was once a pleasure arena in its own right, with fishing, boating and shooting, although in its later years Nor' Loch became stagnant and polluted with dead animals and rubbish.

It is high summer in 1965 and the good people of Edinburgh are taking their ease in West Princes Street Gardens. The deck chairs are out and the ice-creams are on the go, although judging by the amount of clothing being left on, it was one of those July days that offered more in the way of brightness than warmth. Even Robert Louis Stevenson, a famous son of the city, described Edinburgh's summer weather as `shifty and ungential.' The Mound which separates the West and East Gardens was created from the accumulated rubble resulting from the building of the New Town, north of Princes Street. Some familiar landmarks are perched on this artificial hill, including the domed Bank of Scotland and the classically featured National Gallery and Royal Scottish Academy. The scene is a familiar one enough for both residents and visitors, but it has now achieved worldwide exposure, and perhaps a little notoriety, as the opening shot of the film `Trainspotting.' The world of drug addiction seems light years away from the gentle atmosphere of sunlit peace and relaxation captured on this 1965 photograph.

Hearts centre-forward, Willie Bauld, takes on the Newcastle right-back in aerial combat in a 1950 game at Tynecastle. The occasion is an Edinburgh Select XI against Newcastle United. Despite its status as a 'friendly', the match has attracted a large crowd, and no doubt it was a keenly contested affair against a Newcastle side containing players such as Milburn and Robledo. An Edinburgh Select would have been composed of players from both Hearts and Hibs at a time when they were both powerhouses in the Scottish game, achieving many honours in the 20 years after the war. For most of the rest of their histories, silverware has been 'thin on the ground,' although Hearts had another great period, between 1890 and 1914, when they won the championship twice and the Scottish Cup four times. Heart of Midlothian was formed in 1873 and Hibernian in 1875, but 125 years later finds the city of Edinburgh languishing behind Glasgow, Aberdeen and Dundee in terms of honours won. What might have been achieved if the clubs had combined? Most of the fans of both clubs would reply that the mixing of the colours maroon and green produces a pretty sickly result - and there's your answer.

**Right:** After the hardships and deprivations of World War II, attendances at sporting events were huge, as people seemed determined to make up for lost time. This is reflected in the vast crowd to be seen at this Murrayfield international against `the auld enemy' in 1948, and anticipation is high as the ball runs loose near the English try line. Exactly one hundred years earlier, Scotland's first senior rugby match was played, between Edinburgh Academicals and a university team. The game involved 50 players and lasted four days! Murrayfield was opened in 1924, replacing Inverleith as the venue for internationals. Whilst the essence of the game, or the passions it arouses, have changed little since this 1948 scene, a great deal else has. The sight of invalids and injured war veterans seated close to the touchline, with rugs over their knees, is now but a memory. Standing in the open air was the option for the majority then, whereas now Murrayfield offers and all-covered venue for seated crowds of up to 67,000. The modern blue warpaint, or flags draped around torsos, are conspicuously absent from this 1948 crowd, and the lone police sergeant can enjoy the game without too many worries about the crowd.

**Below:** The huge Tynecastle crowd gasps as Younger of Hibernian tips a shot from Wardhaugh of Hearts against the post. The names will enable those with long footballing memories to give an approximate date to the action. The exact date was 1950, a time when sporting events of all kinds were drawing massive attendances after the austerity and hardship of the war years. A lack of modern safety regulations also allowed football clubs to pack in crowds of staggering proportions, and this would especially be the case for an Edinburgh derby. The 20 years after the war were halcyon days for both Hearts and Hibs. In this time Hearts won the championship twice, the League Cup twice and the Scottish Cup in 1956. Within 10 years of 1945, Hibernian won three championships. Success in soccer may well depend upon a solid defence, but those who look back fondly to those golden years will doubtless think instantly of the `Terrible Trio' of Hearts forwards - Conn, Bauld and Wardaugh - or the `Famous Five' Hibernian marauders of Smith, Johnstone, Reilly, Turnbull and Ormond. The decision as to which was the best strike force rests on whether you view the game through maroon or green spectacles.

**Above:** The impressive classical facade of Register House, along with its distinctive dome, is pictured here in 1963. It is situated opposite North Bridge and the Balmoral Hotel, and houses the Scottish Record Office. Built between 1774 and 1827, mainly from designs by Edinburgh educated Robert Adam, its principal function is to `preserve and provide access to our national archival heritage.` Hence, written records dating back to the twelfth century, concerning Scotland, are lodged there. Government, church and legal records are to be found there, as well as estate and family documents. Not that the inside of Register House has not known its lighter moments - literally. In 1784 the intrepid James Tytler, a local journalist, made the first manned hot air balloon ascent on the British mainland, taking off from the Comely Garden. Prior to this, he had practised the inflation of his `Great Fire Balloon' within the shell of a Register House which was then under construction. A few years later, a statue of the Duke of Wellington was erected in front of the steps. Not a man for paperwork, he appears to be perpetually urging his restless horse away from Register House - towards action!

**Above right:** The thousands of bound volumes from which the `Iron Duke' appears to be fleeing act as a magnet for researchers of all kind. The Register House is a treasure trove for students of law, history, religion and politics, or for those who simply wish to track down some personal family history. The records not only date back to the twelfth century, but are constantly

being added to. This 1966 scene reflects the quiet and studious atmosphere one usually finds in such research rooms as the students pore over weighty tomes. Probably the main difference between now and then is the transferring of much archival material onto microfilm. Much can be stored on one small reel, handy to use, and irreplaceable written material can be saved from the wear and tear of constant handling. It is intriguing to speculate about what our earnest students of 1966 were looking into. Was it some such dusty topic as medieval land inheritance, or the more sensational legal case of Burke and Hare in the 1820s? Finding it a profitable business to supply fresh corpses for medical anatomy lessons, they cut out the grave plundering bit by murdering no less than 16 people.

Mention 'theatre' and 'Edinburgh,' and the temptation is to think of the Festival in August. Certainly the number of productions put on at this time is staggering, but residents of the city know, of course, that the live theatre is alive and well the year round, with several theatres presenting professional productions. One of these, the King's Theatre in Leven Street, is pictured here in 1969. Opened in 1906, it has a pleasant Edwardian frontage of red sandstone. Even in those heady days of the live theatre its owners were soon in financial difficulties, and King's fell into the hands of the Howard and Wyndham Company, who made the ever popular pantomime the mainstay of the theatre. The publicity for the Teatro Comunale Florence, as seen outside the theatre in 1969, indicates the theatre's involvement in other areas, notably touring plays and musicals, whilst opera is often the order of the day during the Festival. King's Theatre stands at the end of a long line of rich theatre history in Edinburgh, beginning on the indoor tennis court at Holyrood. A Master of Revels was appointed in the seventeenth century, and the legendary Sarah Siddons trod the boards of the Theatre Royal in 1784.

The expressions on the faces of these men look a little more serious than those usually adopted by soldiers on parade. The photograph dates from around 1929, and possibly shows part of a Remembrance Day ceremony. It had not been much more than a decade earlier, on November 11th 1918, that the guns had finally fallen silent on `the war to end all wars.' The service and parades to commemorate the fallen were much bigger than their modern counterparts, and large crowds assembled on the streets, for nearly everyone could count a family member, or a friend, or an acquaintance amongst the fallen. The particular body of men solemnly marching past here belonged to the Officers' Training Corps of Edinburgh University. Almost 1000 former students had been killed in the Great War, many of them ex-members of the OTC. Around this time, a student could join any one of four units of the OTC - the Battery (the oldest Artillery OTC in Britain), the Engineers, the Infantry, or the Medical Corps. Students being ever much the same not all of them joined with a military career in mind. Some enlisted in the OTC for the adventure and fresh air of the annual summer camp.

# Wartime

*Below: It is difficult to know which to admire most in this wonderful picture of 1934, the engineering magnificence of the Forth Bridge or the graceful shapes of the Hawker Harts. However, it was just as well that 603 Squadron was equipped with Spitfires by the time of the German attack near the bridge on October 16th 1939. Edinburgh's own squadron, 603 of the Royal Auxiliary Air Force, was formed in 1925 and based at Turnhouse. The attack was the first air assault of the war on the British Isles. There seem to be conflicting views about the raid to this day, but the generally accepted version is that four German bombers were brought down, three of them by fighters and one by anti-aircraft fire. A 603 Squadron Spitfire takes the credit for the first German bomber to be brought down over Britain. Fifteen men of the Royal Navy were killed as the Junkers 88s attacked shipping in the Forth, including Commander R F Jolly of the destroyer, `Mohawk.' The Forth continued to see plenty of action. In the summer of 1940 a local coaster, the `Highlander,' shot down two German planes, steaming into Leith with the wing of one of them on its deck.*

Prepared for anything, Mr Bob Williamson stands outside his Anderson Shelter at Comely Bank in 1939. World War II caused terrible fears about bombing, and the government feared that the early days of the war would result in a very high number of casualties. Air raid shelters were dug in East Princes Street Gardens whilst many factories and schools had their own constructed. They were also built on streets, or households could enjoy their own `luxurious' accommodation by buying Anderson Shelters. These were dug deep into gardens, leaving a semi-circle of corrugated metal, reinforced by sandbags, above ground. Each one had six bunks. The problem for Edinburgh folk was the presence of so many underground springs, and the shelters tended to become waterlogged. The most comfortable resident of the one pictured was, apparently, a pet toad! In the event, the shelters were not extensively used because Edinburgh escaped relatively lightly from wartime bombing. Bombs fell near the Forth Bridge on October 16th 1939 in the first air attack of the war on Britain. Another 14 raids were experienced, with 20 deaths and 210 injuries. On one occasion residents poured into the streets with empty jugs when it was heard that the brewery on Russell Road had been hit!

> *Anderson Shelters were dug deep into gardens leaving only a semi-circle of corrugated metal above ground*

**Above:** An amazing display of rifles, helmets and other pieces of military equipment in the window of this Edinburgh store, shows that Britain may have been alone in 1940, but she was not forgotten. Even after Dunkirk and the fall of France, in June 1940, Britain was determined to fight on against Nazi Germany. Although the USA did not join the war until December 1941, there were plenty of people there who admired Britain's stance, and tried to help in any way they could. Hence the window display and the prominent poster, `From Friends in the USA.' The message at the front, to the left, states that a farmer had sent a shotgun, expressing the hope that, `this gun will help some British farmer to protect his home.' The rifles were probably of World War I vintage, and the helmets most certainly were, including German and French ones. Nevertheless, the Local Defence Volunteers, or Home Guard, were glad of anything at this stage, armed as they sometimes were with little more than pikes and clubs.

A photograph in the window shows some of Edinburgh's Home Guard examining the American equipment. Better weapons were soon to be sent, including Browning automatic rifles and Sten guns.

**Below:** There were all manner of shortages and rationing in the Edinburgh of 1939 - 1945. Luxuries disappeared (to pop up again on the `black market') and necessities were restricted in supply. Had you consulted the women of Edinburgh as to whether they regarded make-up as a luxury or a necessity, then perhaps this photograph of a store window in 1940 would have given you the answer. Whether going into uniform, or into the factory, Gala was going to ensure that their customers received `Good Grooming with Economy' - a basic minimum make-up within the war-time restrictions. The emphasis was on lipstick, with `Boulevard' for the Auxiliary Territorial Service, `Ember' for the Women's Auxiliary Air Force and `Lido' for the Women's Royal Naval Service. There was a choice of four for factory and leisure, all of them suggesting a hint of the glamorous and exotic which helped to lift the gloom of those war years. After all, something was needed, what with food rationing and utility clothing that limited pleats and embroidery. The home-made sweets created out of cocoa and sugar were edible, but the ice-cream has been likened to `chilled porridge.'

**Above:** Newbattle Abbey Training Centre is the likely location for this shot of a cheerful group of the Auxiliary Territorial Service during World War II. Women had become more closely involved in the war effort during World War I. Demands on manpower for the front line were so enormous that women had worked in munitions factories, taken on `men's' jobs elsewhere and swollen the ranks of the nursing profession. By the time of the second world war, however, auxiliary units for women had been set up for all the branches of the armed services, and women got into military uniform. The ATS Training Centre at Newbattle Abbey was visited by the Queen and Princess Elizabeth in September 1944, and both took a keen interest in the work going on there. Training included a nine week emergency cookery course, starting with meals for three, and concluding with large-scale field cookery. The Queen and Princess Elizabeth chatted informally with a number of the girls. Clearly many regarded their new lives as an opportunity to broaden their horizons and seek some adventure, for they expressed a wish to go overseas with the army of occupation.

There is more than usual pride in the step of 2603 (City of Edinburgh) Regiment Squadron as it marches down Queensferry Road in 1957, for at `eyes right' is what might be termed their spiritual home at 25 Learmonth Terrace. This humble address has been the headquarters of a number of City of Edinburgh squadrons and units since 1925. The concept of a Reserve Air Force was laid down by Lord Trenchard over 80 years ago, and the house was purchased by the War Ministry to become the Town Headquarters of No 603 (City of Edinburgh) Bomber Squadron in 1925. This was the first Auxiliary Unit to occupy the house, and it was formed on October 14th of that year. The house itself was of a quality to suit the aspirations of those who occupied it. It was, and remains, one of the finest preserved neo-Georgian houses in Scotland. If a proud occasion, the 1957 parade was also a sad one, for it marked the disbandment of 2603 Regiment Squadron, a unit which had provided trained and qualified gunners, signallers, drivers, despatch riders, cooks, storemen, clerks and medical orderlies.

**Both pictures:** With absolute precision the men of 603 (City of Edinburgh) Squadron, Royal Auxiliary Air Force, wheel left on Princes Street (bottom). The crowd is dense behind the barriers, and a mounted policeman sees to it that the cyclists (and even the buses) keep at a respectful distance. The photograph below right shows the same body of men parading their Squadron Standard across Waverley Bridge, and giving a smart `eyes left' to the Lord Provost of Edinburgh.

Both photographs capture a ceremonial occasion of some moment in 1957. Large crowds reflect the public interest, for few sights are more stirring than a uniformed parade, particularly when accompanied by a military band. This parade was, however, a more poignant one than most, for it marked the disbandment of 603 (City of Edinburgh) Squadron, just 12 years after the end of World War II. Such units had shown their worth in this conflict, and the decision to disband was no doubt regretted by many. Certainly the people of Edinburgh gathered to give a rousing farewell, and in so doing showed how close to their hearts was 603 Squadron. The strong link with the people of Edinburgh was in no small measure due to the fact that the headquarters of the Squadron was at 25 Learmonth Terrace, set in the heart of the city. This was very much part of Lord Trenchard's vision, over 80 years ago, for a Reserve Air Force in which

yeomanry units were recruited and trained within their areas of work and residence. Strong identities with their localities could thus be established. Both the Bomber and Fighter Squadrons of 603 had their headquarters at number 25, along with support unit 2603 (Light AA Regiment Unit) and 3603 (Fighter Control Unit). The Edinburgh link with the Royal Auxiliary Air Force remains today at 25 Learmonth Terrace, for it became the Maritime Headquarters Unit in 1959, made up of members from the disbanded 603 Squadron and 3603 (Fighter Control Unit). A memorial plaque to 603 Squadron was erected in March 1957 opposite the gates of RAF Turnhouse before its closure. Yet another memorial is a full-scale fibreglass replica of a Spitfire at Edinburgh Airport.

# Around the city centre

The junction of Princes Street with Lothian Road presents a busy scene in March 1966, with some of the vehicles on view bound to rekindle a few memories amongst those who made their first `hiccuping' efforts behind the wheel in that decade. Apart from that, the aspect remains very much the same today, with the Castle making its dominating presence felt. Such a natural defensive site as this volcanic `plug' of rock could not be missed, and a fortress has stood there since the earliest times. However, it may have been from the Northumbrian King Edwin,

*A fortress has stood on the 'rock' since the earliest times*

who built a strong fortress here in the sixth century, that the city took its name. Equally dominating in the foreground is St Cuthbert's Church, although a decorative feature of St John's is just peeping in to the left. St Cuthbert's has a history dating back to the seventh century. This may make it the oldest place of Christian worship in Edinburgh, even though most of the existing building dates back only to 1894. A curious feature in the churchyard is a cylindrical watchtower, erected in 1827, in an attempt to curb the plague of that time - stealing new corpses from graves to sell for medical research!

**Above:** The cobbled area of the Grassmarket, as pictured in 1966, presents the old cheek-by-jowl with the new. The traditional tenements of the Old Town, with their crow-stepped gables, are a solid reminder of Edinburgh's past. The rather nifty looking sports car parked outside Paul Couts Ltd, retailer of antique furniture, is perhaps a glimpse of the future. The tenements of Old Town evolved from the pressure of a growing population on the labyrinth of narrow wynds and closes that made up seventeenth century Edinburgh. Lack of space meant that expansion could only be upwards, storey upon storey. The result was a rich social mix and the growth of turbulence. The city became infamous for its lawless mobs and its street brawls, or `tulzies.' Grassmarket was the scene of the Porteous Riots in 1736 in which the unfortunate Captain Porteous, commander of the city guard, was hanged from a dyer's pole. During the 1880s, when the Forth Bridge workers lodged in the Old Town tenements, the police patrolled the Grassmarket in sixes. By this time the wealthy had long since decamped to the elegant New Town, perhaps to make a shadowy return in recent years with the slow `gentrification' of Old Town.

**Below:** Although much may have changed in Edinburgh since the date of this photograph, 1951, the Castle speaks of durability and continuity. This applies even more to the ancient volcanic rock on which it stands. This has changed little since the grinding of ice sculpted it into its present shape - perhaps a million years ago. As for the volcanic rock itself, we are talking of a timespan that is almost incomprehensible - around 350 million years. The defensive possibilities of the rock are clear to be seen, and this has meant human occupation from at least the ninth century BC. The resulting fortresses have been squabbled over for centuries, and the rock was in the hands of Northumbrian kings for around 400 years, until Michael Canmore took the castle for his new Kingdom of Scotland in 1018. Since that time the ebb and flow of history has seen the English in occupancy again, once under Cromwell; the birth of a future King of England there, James I, in 1566; the repulse of the Young Pretender (1745); and even a Zeppelin attack, in 1916.

This aerial photograph of 1971 gives some perspective to this part of central Edinburgh in that features mentioned in other photographs may be seen in relation to each other. The best reference point to begin with is to follow the line of Shandwick Place from the bottom left. It links in to Princes Street, almost in the centre, which then bisects the photograph to the right. Below Princes Street, the greenery and parkland of the Gardens are visible. Above Princes Street, the long parallel lines of George Street and Queen Street indicate the gridiron pattern of New Town,

an ambitious building programme which began in 1767. The quiet, private gardens of Queen Street stand out clearly. George Street progresses towards the left into the greenery of exclusive Charlotte Square, and at the edge of the picture is the dome of West Register House. Much of the bottom right of the picture, below Lothian Road, shows the swathe that was created by the demolition of Princes Street Station in 1965. Near the junction of Lothian Road and Princes Street stands the magnificent Caledonian Hotel, built of red Dumfriesshire sandstone and opened in 1903.

This aerial shot from the west was taken in 1965, the very year that Princes Street station, at the junction of Lothian Road and Rutland Street, was closed down. The long rake of station buildings can be seen in the foreground, behind the Caledonian Hotel. To the left of the hotel, the churches of St John and St Cuthbert mark the western end of Princes Street, the line of which stretches up the photograph to the impressive shapes of the Royal Scottish Academy and the National Gallery of Scotland. Beyond these are the Waverley and North Bridges and, in the

distance, the Forth. It is strange to think that the greenery and gardens flanking Princes Street, beneath the castle, are the site of what was once Nor' Loch, a stagnant stretch of water polluted by rubbish and dead animals. The Loch was drained over a period of 60 years from around 1759, allowing Princes Gardens to be established and the concept of Edinburgh's New Town to proceed. The top part of the photograph belongs to Arthur's Seat and Salisbury Crags, and a view such as this shows just how very much this rugged mass makes its presence felt.

As with so many views of Edinburgh, this aerial one of 1971, looking north, finds the Castle dominating the scene. Princes Street and Lothian Road form almost a right-angle as they give a picture frame effect to the shot, at least on two sides. The geometrical effect is enhanced as the eye moves northward into New Town with its planned rectangular shapes of the late eighteenth and early nineteenth century. The long and straight George Street and Queen Street, parallel to Princes Street, are neatly bisected by Hanover, Frederick and Castle

*Usher Hall has the city's largest auditorium, with 2,900 seats*

Streets. The area to the bottom of the photograph, roughly south and east of the Castle, is Edinburgh's Old Town, with all signs of a more organic, unplanned growth, much of it upwards into tenement buildings. Johnston Terrace skirts the hill beneath the castle. Then one moves south through Grassmarket and on to Heriot's School. To the right of this is the university area. To the left of the picture, a distinctive feature is the domed roof of Usher Hall, close to Lothian Road. This is the city's largest hall, with a 2,900 seat auditorium. It was opened in 1914.

**Below:** Although trapped in shadow, this 1966 shot captures the plaque on the wall, above the sign for Guthrie Street, marking this as the birthplace of Sir Walter Scott. Scott was born in 1771, and it is fitting that the birthplace of a man who had such an enormous influence on the culture of his day should be surrounded by such cultural sites as the Edinburgh and Heriot-Watt Universities, and the Royal Museum of Scotland. Scott's fame rests on his reputation as a poet and novelist, especially the exploration of Scotland's romantic past in his Waverley novels. He was, however, not merely a literary man, but also an active patriot. It was he who, in 1817, discovered the royal regalia locked away in the Castle and had it put on display. This comprised a royal crown, sword and

sceptre dating back to at least the sixteenth century. Scott also organised the state visit of George IV to Holyrood in 1822, ensuring that all wore Highland dress. Scott's work, which sadly is no longer in fashion, is commemorated in Lady Stair's House, Lawnmarket. Also, some of his fictional creations have been immortalised in the names of locomotives, stations and ships.

**Bottom:** Surely this must be one of the most instantly recognisable shapes in the world, the Forth Bridge, photographed from the air in 1949. In the late nineteenth century, when practically all the commerce of Britain was carried by rail, the directors of four railway companies appointed Thomas Bouch to design a structure to span the Forth. The collapse of the Tay Bridge, designed by Bouch, brought a hasty change of plan. Ultimately the designers, Benjamin Baker and John Fowler, set to work and produced one of the engineering wonders of the world. After seven years of effort, the Forth Bridge was opened in 1890, with its three huge cantilevers supporting a viaduct across a distance of 2,582 metres. The bridge has always produced statistics of mammoth proportions - two-thirds of a million cubic feet of Aberdeen granite; 54,000 tons of steel; the enduring story of endless painting. However, as in so many other cases, the sum is greater than its parts. It is the overall impression of the bridge, with its magnificent symmetry, which stays in the mind. Yet again, that familiar image might instantly evoke the filmed version of Buchan's `The 39 Steps,' with Richard Hannay crouching amongst the girders and dodging express trains.

**Below:** Like Rome, the city of Edinburgh was built on or around seven hills, and this panoramic shot was taken from the 98 metre high Calton Hill, in 1960. This was in the pre-stone cleaning era, before some of the more distinguished buildings were to emerge again in their original glory, and the disfiguring grime is very apparent. Nevertheless, the eye is drawn along Waterloo Place towards Princes Street and the imposing North British Hotel, almost in the centre of the photograph. Opened in 1902 by the North British Railway Company, the 55 metre clock tower (with a clock traditionally kept two minutes fast) has been an Edinburgh landmark ever since. Sold by the railway into private hands in 1981, the building was re-opened as the Balmoral Hotel in 1991. The bulk of the Castle area rears up to the left of the old North British, whilst almost at the extremity is the tall spire of the Tollbooth Kirk. The large building in the foreground, to the left, is the civil service headquarters, St Andrew's House, built on the site of the former Calton Hill Gaol. Just to the rear of this is the old Burial Ground, with the distinctive North Bridge also making an appearance.

**Right:** A wonderful vista, as viewed from the North British Hotel in 1960, encompasses much of Edinburgh's finest urban scenery. From Waverley Station, bottom left, the railway lines snake past East Princes Street Gardens to vanish beneath the Mound. As if Edinburgh has not enough natural hills, this one was created out of the rubble from the New Town excavations, around 1820. The National Gallery of Scotland, still with a rather grubby exterior in 1960, sits atop the Mound, with the Royal Scottish Academy to its right. The area around these galleries is Edinburgh's version of Hyde Park Corner in the context of soap-box oratory. During the Festival there is never a dull moment in this vicinity - from string quartets to fire-eaters - a free festival of fun. The foreground to the right is dominated by the monument to Sir Walter Scott, completed in 1846. This Gothic spire, 60 metres high, may seem over elaborate to modern taste, but it was created very much in the ebullient spirit of Victorian times, and should be judged in that light. In the background, features that may easily be picked out are the Castle, the imposing Caledonian Hotel, the tall spire of St Mary's Cathedral and the dome of West Register House.

Thomas Carlyle described this vista as `the finest city prospect in the World.' Admittedly, as a border Scot he may have been a little biased, but this wonderful view along Princes Street does something to support his claim. Princes Street was completed in 1805 as part of the New Town scheme, and was named after Prince George, later George IV. Its distinction lies not so much in its width, nor in its mile long straightness, but in the panorama of trees, gardens and distinguished buildings which flank the south side. In the foreground, at the junction with Lothian Road, stands the nineteenth century church of St John with, to the right, the church of St Cuthbert and its tower of 1789. At the far end of Princes Street the clock tower of the North British Hotel (now the Balmoral) and the Scott Memorial are both prominent, and somewhat closer can be seen the gleaming, classical shapes of the National Gallery and the Royal Scottish Academy. The north side of Princes Street is nowhere near as scenic, but the clock at Binns (bottom left) may bring back happy memories to some. It was a favourite rendezvous spot for courting couples when this photograph was taken, in 1965.

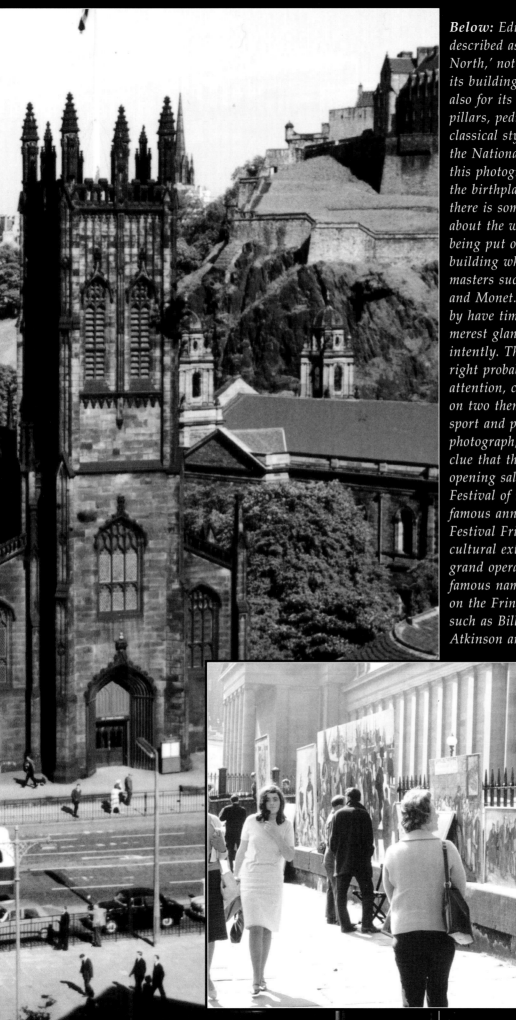

**Below:** Edinburgh was once famously described as `the Athens of the North,' not just for the abundance of its buildings in classical style, but also for its cultural traditions. The pillars, pediments and porticos of the classical style are well represented by the National Gallery of Scotland in this photograph. Also, if Athens was the birthplace of modern democracy, there is something very democratic about the work of amateur artists being put on display alongside a building which houses the works of masters such as Rembrandt, Titian and Monet. As always, some passers-by have time for no more than the merest glance, whilst others gaze intently. The two paintings on the right probably attracted plenty of attention, concentrating as they did on two themes beloved of most Scots - sport and politics! The date of the photograph, August 1965, gives the clue that this was probably an opening salvo in the Edinburgh Festival of that year. This world famous annual event, along with the Festival Fringe, presents a three week cultural extravaganza ranging from grand opera to street theatre. Many famous names have made their débuts on the Fringe, especially comedians such as Billy Connolly, Rowan Atkinson and Harry Hill.

**Above:** The Royal Mile, stretching from Castle Hill to Holyroodhouse, contains an incredible amount of history. Before the building of New Town, it was the heart of Edinburgh life - noisy, smelly, crowded and turbulent. Dominating the right-hand side of this 1960 shot are the pinnacles of Tolbooth St John's, the `Highland Church.' From the bottom of Castle Hill, the Lawnmarket stretches straight ahead. Within this area was the eighteenth century home of the notorious Deacon Brodie, a respectable town councillor by day and a ruthless thief by night. He was hanged in 1788, and gave Robert Louis Stevenson the inspiration for his creation of `Dr Jekyll and Mr Hyde.' High Street then takes over from Lawnmarket, the most prominent feature being the fine crown topping the square tower of St Giles Cathedral, more properly known as the High Kirk of Edinburgh. It was here, in 1637, that Jenny Geddes hurled her stool at the preacher in protest at the English inspired new prayer book. The Tron Church, to the left of St Giles, has become the traditional meeting place of Hogmanay revellers. The `tron' itself was once a weighbeam to which merchants were nailed by their ears if their weights were wrong!

**Right:** A busy and sunlit day in 1962 finds Princes Street thronged. The vehicles on view will be a treat for connoisseurs, with some in the nostalgia category (the Mini, the Morris Minor) if not quite in the vintage class. As for the pedestrians, there appears to be too much hurry and scurry about the scene for this to be traditional Princes Street promenading, whereby generations of Edinburgh young folk have strolled along, seeking to catch the eye of the opposite sex. If any of the throng are seeking a genuine public house, however, Princes Street is not the place to find it. Rose Street, the narrow thoroughfare just behind, is the place for a quenching of the thirst. The foreground of the picture is dominated by the intricacies of the 60 metre high Scott Monument, with the great man sitting pensively within. The Monument incorporates three Scottish monarchs, 16 poets and 64 of Scott's characters, along with a 287 step staircase to the top. The whole concept stemmed from the creativity of a Peebleshire carpenter, George Meikle Kemp, who had won the design competition. Tragically, Kemp did not see his design come to full fruition in 1846. He was drowned in the Union Canal in 1844.

Crossing over from Princes Street or Waterloo Place into the older part of Edinburgh city centre is like entering another world. Gone is the elegant, if rather formal, architecture of New Town, to be replaced by an intriguing mosaic of styles. The subject of this photograph of 1969, John Knox's House in High Street, is a wonderful example. It gives the appearance not so much as having been built, as having grown gradually, with little bits tacked on in the course of time. And this is exactly what happened, with a fifteenth century bottom section, a sixteenth century middle storey and an early seventeenth century top part -three houses in one! The initials of one of the earliest owners, Mariota Arres, and those of her husband James Mosman, may still be seen on the wall outside. Whether John Knox ever lived there is debatable, but in its role as a museum it contains interesting material relating to his life. It was Knox's fiery preaching in St Giles, in the 1560s, which was at the heart of the Scottish Reformation. He is perhaps best known for his thundering denunciations of the Catholic, Mary Queen of Scots, as a leading member of the 'monstrous regiment of women.'

**Above:** St Andrew's Church (now the Church of St Andrew and St George) presents an image of tranquillity in the late afternoon sunshine of a spring day in 1960, and it is difficult to imagine the turbulent scenes that were once enacted within. St Andrew's was built between 1782 and 1785 to a design by Andrew Fraser, and the steeple was added in 1789. It was the first church to be built in New Town, that self-conscious attempt between 1767 and 1840 to create a world-class city fit to rank alongside such as Vienna. The original driving force was the Lord Provost of Edinburgh, George Drummond, and the names of the new streets - Hanover, Cumberland, George etc - were statements of the city's loyalty to the Hanoverian dynasty. The neo-classical style of architecture adopted is well represented by St Andrew's, on George Street, with its

solid columns and triangular pediment. In 1843, however, harmony of style was not reflected by religious harmony. In this year came the `Great Disruption,' when Thomas Chalmers led 450 ministers out of St Andrew's, and out of the Church of Scotland, to found what they considered to be the more democratic Free Church of Scotland.

**Top:** The Armstrong Siddely says it all. There is not much of the elegant Georgian architecture of Charlotte Square on view in this 1956 photograph, but the beautiful motor car gives the same message - wealth and gracious living. Charlotte Square is the epitome of New Town, four square miles of wide streets along with spacious crescents and squares, laid out in grid-iron pattern. This astonishing experiment in town planning was aimed at putting Edinburgh alongside the foremost cities of Europe. A competition in 1766 produced a planner, a precocious 23 year old named James Craig. The scheme went speedily ahead, and by the end of the century the most notable buildings of New Town were in place, built in neo-classical style out of sandstone. Charlotte Square was designed by Robert Adam, its north side being recognised as a masterpiece. Numbers five to seven, formerly the property of the Marquess of Bute, came into the hands of the National Trust for Scotland in 1966, and number seven has been restored as a Georgian period piece. New Town sucked in the gentry and assets of Old Town, and the concentration of wealth there continues, with Charlotte Square as the heart of Edinburgh's important financial community.

# In sickness and in health

**Below:** Corstophine is probably best known as a pleasant wooded hill whose healthy and bracing atmosphere was considered highly suitable for the location of a convalescent home there by the Edinburgh Royal Infirmary in the nineteenth century. These young mothers pictured at Costorphine Clinic in 1966 perhaps had a headstart for their babies in terms of the healthy air of the hill, but regular monitoring of a baby's progress was as vital then as it is now. It's a cheerful scene at the clinic as the nurse weighs a baby, with proud mum looking on. No doubt the mothers of 1966 had the same anxieties as mothers today about how their little ones would cope with the triple vaccination against diphtheria, tetanus and whooping cough. However, the anti-polio drops were given on a sugar lump in those days - much frowned upon now. The surroundings look a little less comfortable in 1966, and the walls seem less plastered with warnings against smoking and invitations to post-natal classes. Any local clinic has one other important function apart from the official advice and help, and that is for mothers to meet each other socially and perhaps set up their own mutually supportive networks.

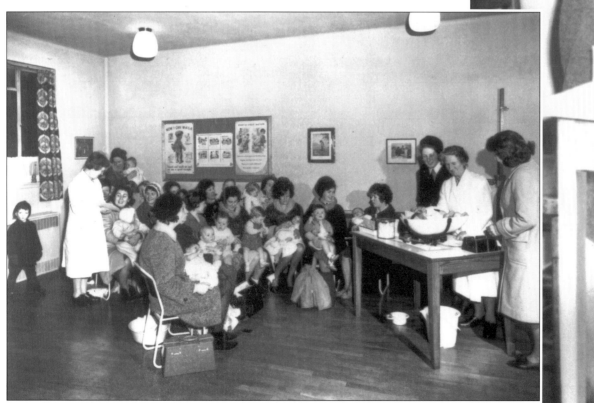

From the founding of the National Health Service in 1948, the local clinic has been seen as the focal point for routine help and advice for mothers and children. This 1966 scene from Corstophine Clinic shows a line of mothers collecting welfare foods for their babies and infants, with no doubt a few words of advice thrown in. The concept of this type of infant welfare really expanded during World War II, when wholesale shortages due to enemy `U'-boat activity made the government come up with alternative strategies for raising healthy youngsters. Powdered milk and concentrated vitamin mixtures were made available free to all. Some readers might remember that spoonful of cod-liver oil, only made bearable by the delicious concentrated orange-juice which followed. The familiar tins of National Dried Milk can be seen on the table in the 1966 shot, along with the health-giving bottles. What is also visible is the 60s poster which has become a kind of classic - `Coughs and Sneezes Spread Diseases.' The main differences between now and then are that the vitamins come in droplet form, ready for adding to a drink, and they are no longer `free to all.'

**Bottom:** The Simpson Memorial Hospital of the Royal Infirmary, built in 1879, had come under great pressure by the 1920s. With only 94 beds, and an average monthly waiting list of 2,800, the problems were acute. Nevertheless, the difficulty of raising £500,000 to buy land and build new premises was equally problematic at a time when hospitals were heavily reliant upon public subscriptions, charity appeals and bequests. Therefore, it was not until 1939 that the Duchess of Gloucester opened the new Simpson Memorial Maternity Pavilion. It boasted earphones and soft music for the patients, and south facing wards with balconies onto which the beds could be wheeled on nice days. There were also only six beds to a ward, and so the picture is likely to belong to the days of the `old Simpson.' The cots are neatly lined up, ready to wheel the babies in and out of the nursery, for this was well before the time of babies being `roomed in' with their mothers on the wards. Along with this has come a more relaxed atmosphere in maternity wards, and more liberal visiting hours for fathers. The Simpson has continued to grow and develop, and has an enviable reputation for midwifery training.

**Below right:** What a heart-warming sight as this batch of new-born babies savour their first day of life in 1933. Contentment, sadness, puzzlement, resignation - these are some of the expressions that are being registered. Presumably their name-tags were secure and they all arrived at their rightful owners. The sight of babies `en masse' like this is a reminder of the time, up to the late 50s, when babies were kept in the nursery of a maternity hospital, and mothers didn't see a great deal of them at first, except at feeding times. There was no `feeding on demand' either; times were as regular as clockwork. The photograph was taken at the Edinburgh Royal Infirmary and Simpson Memorial Hospital at Lauriston Place, and the featured babies will now be adults in their mid-60s. It is quite a poignant picture in that those babies, who all began life together, will have gone on to lead totally different lives. The Simpson Memorial Hospital was named after Sir James Young Simpson, a staff member of the old Royal Edinburgh Maternity Hospital. Some of the pains of childbirth were eased by this nineteenth century pioneer of anaesthesia, and a statue in tribute to him stands on Princes Street.

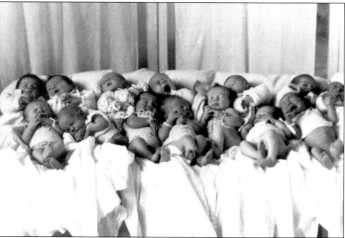

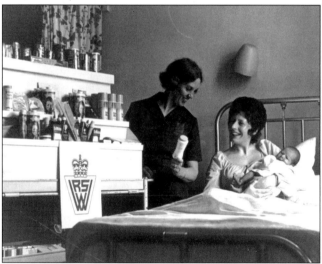

**Above:** `Rooming in' was very much the order of the day by the time this photograph was taken at the Elsie Inglis Memorial Hospital. The proud mum seems delighted to be exchanging `baby care' notes with her visitor from the Women's Royal Voluntary Service, who surely holds the ubiquitous Johnson's Baby Powder in her hand. The WVS only incorporated the word `Royal' into its title in 1966, and so the picture must date from after this, as the emblem on the trolley makes plain. For an organisation that was set up principally to assist in Civil Defence, in 1938, the WVS had found outlets for its energies in a remarkable number of areas by the 1960s. Voluntary work in hospitals was just one of them, with its trolley shops being every popular. Perhaps it was the friendly chat that was the most important part,

especially in the era when mothers stayed in hospital for 10 to 14 days after childbirth, and dads were only allowed to visit for half-an-hour each evening. By 1966, of course, things were much more liberal. Sadly, 1988 saw the end of Elsie Inglis Memorial Hospital when reorganisation meant its closure.

**Top:** The Elsie Inglis Memorial Hospital was founded in the Abbeyhill area in 1925. It must have been one of Edinburgh's kinder days when this charming photograph was taken, for the mums have been wheeled onto the verandah to enjoy the sunshine. The nurses seem to have brought the babies along, so perhaps this indicates a time when the babies were generally kept in nurseries, only visiting their mums for feeding, or for photo calls like this one. `Rooming in,' whereby babies stayed in the wards with their mothers, more or less all the time, generally began to be adopted in the late 50s. The `Elsie Inglis' was a maternity hospital held in great esteem in Edinburgh, its name commemorating the work in the first world war Dr Elsie Inglis. Educated in Edinburgh, she had led field hospital units, almost entirely staffed by women, in France, Serbia and Russia. The British War Office and the Red Cross had refused her offers of service. A pillar of strength in the middle of appalling slaughter, it was a tragic irony that Dr Inglis herself died of cancer in 1917. At her funeral procession along Princes Street, the silent crowds stood eight deep.

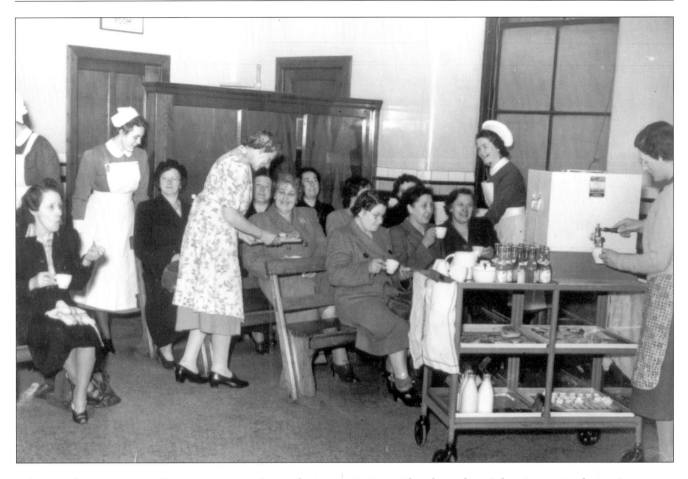

**Above:** The canteen trolley was a popular sight in the Medical Out-Patient Department of the Royal Infirmary, Edinburgh, in 1950. The two volunteers are being kept busy, with the lady on the right slaving away over a hot urn, whilst the lady with the tray dispenses the liquid refreshment and biscuits. Of course a nice cup of tea is welcome at almost any time, but in this case it might have been especially so because there was no appointments system until 1956, and it was a matter of a long wait for most people. The Royal Infirmary was well aware of this defect, and there was also criticism of the mingling of emergency and non-emergency cases. The accommodation was cramped and outdated by 1950, the Out-Patient Department being situated on the ground floor of the old, 1738, George Watson's Hospital Building. There has been a huge improvement in matters since that time, with comfortable consulting `suites' in cheerful surrounding, and specialist Out-Patient Departments in such areas as asthma, haematology and renal medicine. The 1950 scene does look rather `spartan,' but the nurses are doing their best to spread some cheer and there are plenty of smiles in evidence.

**Below:** The thought of the dentist's chair always suggests the prospect of pain, or at least discomfort, and then there is the indignity of lying back with all that ironmongery in your mouth. It must have taken real courage, then, to lie back and know that not just two pairs of eyes were critically examining the defects of your teeth, but nine pairs! The Edinburgh Dental Hospital has won an international reputation, but students have to learn on `live' patients. The photograph shows training in action, but offers a puzzle in that the style of nurse's uniform and a fully reclining chair do not quite seem to fit into the same era. The Edinburgh Dental Dispensary was opened in 1860, in Drummond Street, by John Smith and three friends. John Smith was a pioneer teacher of dental surgery. What became the Dental Hospital and School moved to Chambers Street in 1878 and, with a short break, has remained there ever since. The building was reconstructed and extended in 1953, with further accommodation being found at High School Yards in 1979. The emphasis now is on retention of teeth, wherever possible, whereas up to the 1940s total extraction and false teeth was common practice.

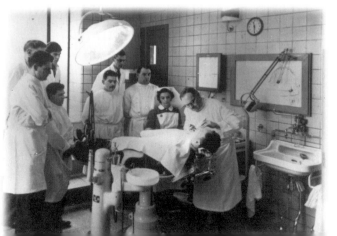

# On the home front

This vacant property in Edinburgh had little chance of being either let or sold once the Women's Voluntary Service had taken it over. The main function of WVS during World War II was in the realms of Civil Defence, particularly in dealing with the consequences of air raids. However, many other tasks were taken on, including the energetic exercise involved in throwing clothing parcels about. In this case, as the notice makes clear, the parcels were destined for His Majesty's Forces. Much of the clothing was knitted by members - seaboot stockings, sweaters, balaclavas and mittens.

One of the most notable achievements was to turn one million pounds of khaki double knitting wool into cap comforters. Over three million garments were mended annually for the Forces. Books and newspapers were also dispatched abroad, or delivered within Britain by mobile libraries and canteens. More in line with its main function, the WVS was appointed sole agent for civilian relief in Britain for the American Red Cross. Millions of garments arrived, from the USA and elsewhere, and it was the job of WVS to distribute these to the bombed-out - a huge undertaking.

**Above:** The early days of World War II brought scenes to Edinburgh that must have seemed like a nightmare come true as, for the first time, civilians were expected to be in the front line. Bombing was the great fear. Pathetic columns of children were being evacuated from Edinburgh even before the official outbreak of war, and air-raid shelters were being dug in Princes Street Gardens. Amidst all the unusual scenes, it was nevertheless quite a shock for the citizens of the city to find a Messerschmitt 109 parked in Princes Street Gardens, and the picture shows the amount of interest that was aroused. The German plane had, in fact, been brought down over Kent, and was being used as publicity for the first big money-raising drive of the conflict, `War Weapons Week.' The Women's Voluntary Service was closely linked with all such campaigns as this, and the photograph shows Lady Ruth Balfour, first WVS Chairman for Scotland, with three fellow members. Later big drives were `Warship Week,' `Wings for Victory' and `Salute the Soldier.' Edinburgh raised a staggering £52,000.000 in the four campaigns. The WVS also spearheaded the drive to collect aluminium for building aeroplanes, collecting 1000 tons in total nationwide.

**Right:** What a wonderful publicity idea to have an actress from the King's Theatre supporting the drive to persuade people to give blood. She is `manning' the Blood Transfusion Advertising Stall in a shot that may date back to the 1940s. Whilst she fastens some sort of sticker to the lapel of the other lady, she is most liberal with her smile. The little Pekinese dog adds that final touch of the exotic, and the label around its neck states, `I am Goldie. It is my birthday.' Giving blood is not only a worthwhile activity, but a necessary one in the cause of saving lives. It is not, however, something that most people readily do. Thankfully, the Tony Hancock type of blood donor is rare, but people often need to be cajoled to some degree. As the notice on the stall stays, `Half-an-hour of your time will give someone else a lifetime. 20,000 more donors needed.' Modern approaches may be more sophisticated, but the message remains the same. Not only that, it was good publicity for King's Theatre!

*Lunch is served as eager diners cluster around the `Scottish Convoy' wagon, officially entitled a Ministry of Food Transportable Kitchen Unit. The occasion was a Civil Defence emergency feeding demonstration, held at Springfield House, Edinburgh, in October 1953. The concept of Civil Defence had emerged just prior to World War II, in the expectation of heavy civilian casualties from enemy bombing, accompanied by a possible breakdown of services. What began as Air-Raid Precaution soon spread to auxiliary fire-fighting and ambulance services, all on a voluntary basis. The post-war years saw the start of the Cold War with Russia, and the prospect of towns and cities being utterly devastated by nuclear weapons. The government felt it important to encourage the continuance of Civil Defence, especially with a pool of trained volunteers already available. Delegates to the Emergency Feeding Conference were given a practical example of just what was meant by this when they saw lunch for 100 people being prepared on improvised brick cookers and on equipment from the Transportable Kitchen Unit.*

**Above:** The awesome sight of a brick cooker `in full cry,' belching forth smoke and steam, is shown in this photograph. It is attended by members of the Women's Voluntary Service, which had been created with Civil Defence very much in mind in 1938. Although the WVS contributed to the 1953 exercise, the bulk of the cooking was done by the Army Catering Corps. About half of the 100 lunches were produced on a combination of brick hot plate ovens and dustbin cookers. The representatives at the conference, who came from a wide area around Edinburgh, then set to work to try the results for themselves. Lunch consisted of brown stew and vegetables, followed by jam tart and custard, and finally coffee and biscuits. It was generally agreed that it was a very good meal, and the Lord Provost of Edinburgh, Sir James Miller, then made a plea to the conference for more publicity and volunteers for Civil Defence. Such emergency feeding schemes as were devised by local authorities, as a result of this conference, fortunately have never yet had to be implemented on the scale that was feared at the time.

**Below:** The chairman of the Women's Voluntary Service in Scotland, Mrs M E Campbell, points out the main features of the famous Forth Bridge to the Lord Mayor of Sydney, Australia, Alderman E C O'Dea. He was visiting the United Kingdom at the end of December 1950 to initiate the distribution of Australia's final gift of 300,000 parcels through the Australian Express Parcel Scheme, which was being wound up that year. The scheme had begun in 1947, since when around three million parcels had been sent, with a total value of around £1,500,000. It says much for the crippling effects of World War II on the British economy that, even after the war, Australia and other Commonwealth countries sent help in this way. Austerity was a fact of life in Britain right up to the early 1950s, and rationing did not entirely disappear until that decade. Alderman O'Dea attended a function at the Usher Hall Edinburgh, where 2000 old-age pensioners each received an Australian food parcel. The Women's Voluntary Service, which had distributed many of the parcels throughout the scheme, acted as host to the visitor, who spoke of the great admiration felt for Britain in Australia, and its determination to share both the joys and adversities of Britain.

**Right:** A huge box of toys lies in the middle of the floor as ladies from the Women's Voluntary Service distribute presents to eager little girls. The photograph dates from the 1940s, and this must have been one of the more pleasant tasks of the WVS, notwithstanding the sad fact that these were sick children. The Royal Edinburgh Hospital for Sick Children, familiarly known as the `Sick Kids,' is world famous for its paediatric knowledge. It owes its existence to two visionary medical men of the nineteenth century, Dr Charles Wilson and Dr John Smith, who began in a small way, in 1860, at 7 Lauriston Lane. The building which forms the heart of the `Sick Kids' today, at Sciennes Road, was built in 1895 with the help of a gift of £10,000 from Lady Jane Dundas. From desperate battles against fevers such as typhoid and scarlatina, the hospital has come a long way. The two founders would have considered such things as open-heart surgery and growth hormone treatment as little short of miraculous. Attitudes too have changed. Between the wars, parents were banned from visiting their children, and from the war to the early 1950s, visits were limited to one a week.

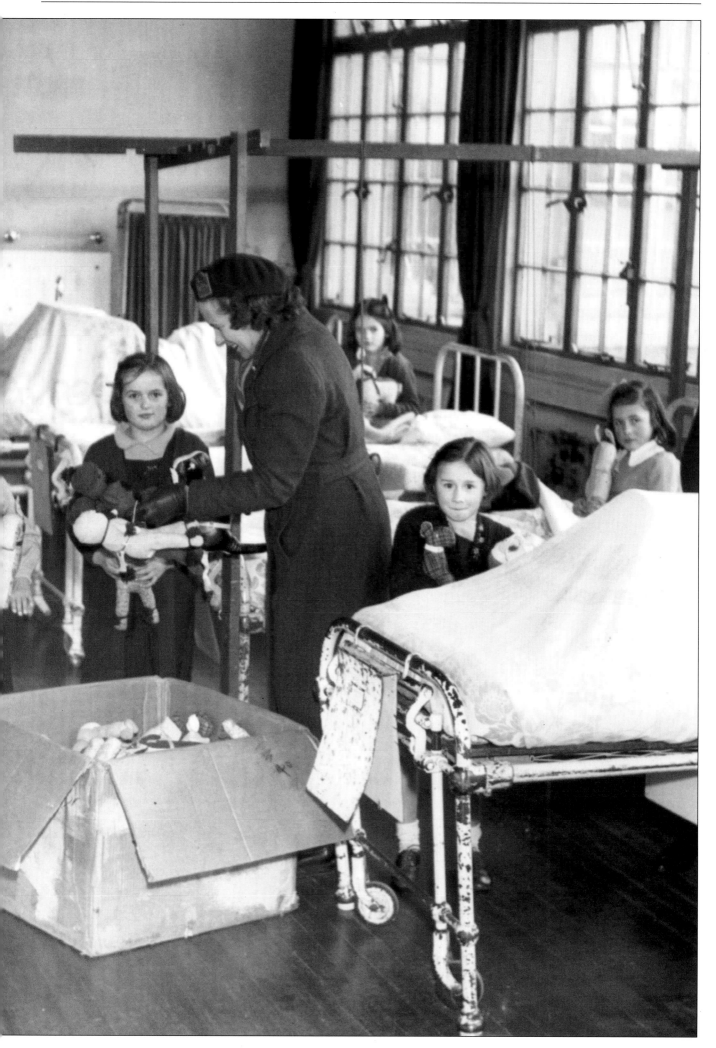

*(Inset) Of all the activities the Women's Voluntary Service has enthusiastically engaged in since its foundation as a Civil Defence auxiliary unit in 1938, it would be difficult to pinpoint the one that is best known to the public. There are so many. `Ask the WVS' has become almost an automatic response to any situation of civilian crisis or of vulnerable people needing attention or care. It is a fair bet, however, that `Meals-on-Wheels' would be high on the list of the public's perception of WVS. The Edinburgh Central members of this worthy organisation are looking delighted at what was probably the acquisition of two spanking new vans in this photograph from the late 50s. The vehicles, entitled `Cowan' and `Hanover,' are gaining the seal of approval from two key figures in WVS, who both stand in front of `Hanover.' On the right is Mrs Marshall, `Meals-on-Wheels' organiser for Edinburgh Central, and on the left is Lady MacColl, Chairman of WVS in Scotland. Things had moved on a long way from the immediate post-war years when members often delivered meals in their own vehicles. (Main picture) Naturally it is the contents of the vans, and not their*

*shine and sparkle, which is of most importance to both the organisers and recipients of `Meals-on-Wheels.' Lady MacColl and Mrs Marshall inspect the neatly stacked metal containers whilst the chefs stand nearby, ready to vouch for the quality of what goes into them. No doubt both ladies sampled the fare for themselves. Women's Voluntary Service had gained much experience in providing emergency meals to civilians during the second world war, often with the most primitive equipment. WVS mobile canteens also operated to serve the troops, both at home and abroad. To distribute `Meals-on-Wheels' on a regular basis to needy people in peacetime was a new challenge, but one that the organisation readily adapted to. In the first six months of 1958, which is the rough date of this photograph, nationwide the WVS delivered 750,000 such meals - the first courses always piping hot from `Hot Lock' containers. Naturally the focus of the service has always been the elderly, and the social benefit has almost been as important as the regular, nourishing meals. Old people are often alone and welcome the little chat with people they have come to regard as friends.*

PSC 257

**Left:** Edinburgh had plenty of international visitors before the second world war, but most of these would have arrived armed with guide books and an itinerary. During the war the city became truly cosmopolitan, with thousands of French, Polish, Norwegian, Dutch, Czech, American and Dominion troops thronging the streets. Many of these were on leave, for Edinburgh was a relatively safe place in terms of bombing. The Women's Voluntary Service Information Bureau in the city did outstanding work in this respect. The first point of contact was Waverley Station, and WVS guides are shown on the photograph greeting visitors and dispensing essential information. The visitors themselves pose somewhat of a mystery, for they look a little on the elderly side to be troops. The Edinburgh Bureau was set up after Dunkirk, in 1940, and by the end of the war it could call upon interpreters in 21 languages. The `downside' to this influx of soldiers was an increase in drunkenness and rowdiness. American GI's seemed to have enough money to buy anything that was going on the `black market,' and the prospect of silk stockings attracted local girls. To the disgruntled Scottish soldiers, the Americans were very definitely `over paid, oversexed and over here.'

**Above:** Eating baked potatoes, and showing every sign of satisfaction, are the Lord Provost of Edinburgh, Sir William Y Darling, along with enthusiastic members of the Women's Voluntary Service. The occasion was a Potato Party to inaugurate Edinburgh Food Week in 1940. The WVS was created in the dark days after the Munich Agreement of 1938, when war seemed more than just a possibility. The grim prospect too was of a war in which civilians would be very much in the `front line,' with bombs raining down on towns and cities. The Home Secretary, Sir Samuel Hoare, approached Lady Reading with a view to recruiting women in air raid precaution work. Starting with a membership of five in September 1938, the WVS was 300,000 strong by the end of the year. Once the war had begun, the WVS turned its hand to anything, including such drives as Edinburgh Food Week. Intense `U'-Boat activity made food shortages a fact of life. Jam, sugar, fat, meat, cheese, eggs - all were rationed. Forward the humble potato, and all other vegetables which could be grown at home in the `Dig for Victory' campaign. Forward too the `interesting' war-time recipes that loyal WVS members tried out on their husbands!

# On the move

**Below:** The bus outside Ritchies Luncheon and Tea Rooms, at 24 Princes Street, was a very special visitor. It was passing through Edinburgh, in February 1928, as part of a six day run through Britain as a promotional stunt to highlight the reliability and endurance of these popular vehicles belonging to Associated Daimler Company. The latter was the product of a brief link between AEC and Daimler, and the destination board shows the initials ADC. The ambitious aim of the exercise was to cover 1830 miles in six days - an incredible achievement (if it was managed) considering that this was well before the age of the by-pass, let alone the motorway. However, narrow and winding though the roads may have been, there was certainly less congestion, and what there was came as much from horse-drawn traffic as from motorcars and buses. The first Edinburgh Corporation bus ran in 1914, and by the 1920s the suburbs were being reached and opened up. Leith was the last area to see horse-drawn buses - in 1909.

*A close-up of the bus belonging to ADC reveals that in 1928 it is receiving as much attention as it would get today, the difference being that then it represented the `cutting edge' of modern bus engineering, whereas today it would be attracting the vintage enthusiasts. The boys at the front are particularly keen, and may be studying the name Associated Daimler engraved at the top of the huge radiator. The registration plate of 319 H would not be raising any eyebrows in 1928, but if any lucky person possessed it today, experts on the transport equivalent of the Antiques Roadshow would be advising them to insure it for about £10,000! The sturdiness of such old vehicles is legendary, and the strength of the bus is echoed by the rear end of the car in front, with its very solid looking hubs. Durability was a necessity at this time, considering the amount of jolting that cobbled or otherwise unsurfaced roads would hand out. The well-dressed people on the pavement may be connected with the bus promotion, or they may simply be queuing for Ritchies Luncheon and Tea Rooms.*

**Right:** This vehicle, powerful and modern for its day, was not part of Edinburgh's public transport system in 1928. It was a migrant visitor on a promotional exercise

for Associated Daimler Company, and it is seen here speeding away on a damp and grey day. Buses are a familiar enough city sight nowadays, but as is suggested by the tram lines and overhead cables on the photograph, the main form of public road transport in 1928 was the tram. Nevertheless, the history of buses in Edinburgh stretched back a long way, and a horse-drawn coach service between Edinburgh and Leith was available as early as 1610, albeit irregular and carrying no more than six passengers. By 1826, stage-coaches were running at 30 minute intervals between Port Hopetown (Lothian Road) and Leith. Horse-drawn buses lingered on to 1909. By this time the petrol engine had arrived, and in 1899 the Edinburgh Autocar Company commenced a Daimler waggonette service. Scottish Motor Traction followed not far behind, in 1905. The first Corporation bus ran in 1914. However, municipal buses were outnumbered by trams until as late as 1952, when the decision was made by Edinburgh Corporation Transport to concentrate urban transport on buses.

**Below:** If London buses come in threes, then Edinburgh trams come in seventeens, or so it appears from this remarkable scene on Princes Street in April 1956. The date is significant, and may go some way towards explaining the photograph, for the tram system was winding down from 1952. By the end of 1956 trams had gone altogether. Quite a few readers may be whisked back to their childhood by the sight of these fine old vehicles in their distinctive maroon and white livery. They might bring back the memory of a meeting or a parting, or of a half-forgotten day out to 'somewhere.' To Edinburgh born Ludovic Kennedy, the nostalgia lay simply in the sounds, 'the whine and rattle as they gathered speed, the driver's low-pitched bell to shoo people out of the way.' Edinburgh's first trams were horse-powered, and began their operations in 1871. The application of artificial power, from 1888, saw Edinburgh adopt an unusual system whereby cables ran down the centre of the tracks. The steam powered cable system was not fully converted to a more orthodox electric system until 1923. Thousands watched the last tram make its final journey to Shrubhill Depot on November 16th 1956.

# Shopping spree

Jenners in all its ornate magnificence is captured here during extension work in 1966. It might be overdoing it to call it a 'wondrous Renaissance compilation,' as one awestruck commentator did, but it certainly gives the appearance of having stepped straight from the pages of some book of fantasy fairy tales. The shop that Charles Jenner and Charles Kennington originally opened paid an annual rent of £150. This was in 1838, and the expansion of what was essentially a ladies' fashion store went well until disaster struck in 1892. On November 26th, late at night, a fire ignited in the basement, and the vacuum of the lift hoist soon drew the fire upwards until flames were shooting out of the roof of the four-storey building. The 120 'out-of-town' workers, who were accommodated in two dormitories, were safely evacuated, but the building was destroyed. Within three years a new one was erected out of Aberdeen granite and yellow freestone from Northumberland, the one that we see today. It was designed by W Hamilton Beattie, and its superbly decorated frontage was deliberately intended to resemble Oxford's Bodleian Library - an idea of Charles Jenner. At the grand re-opening, in 1895, 25,000 people visited on the first day.

When the original Jenners store was destroyed by fire in 1892, Charles Jenner had a hand in the design of the new building which utterly transformed the corner of Princes Street and South St David Street. Sadly, he died before the grand re-opening in 1895, but this 1930s photograph shows his particular influence. Women were, in his words, `the support of the house,' the solid basis of the success of Jenners. His tribute to them was to have six pairs of female figures, or caryatids, incorporated into the frontage of the new building, and some of these can clearly be seen to the left of the picture. This was taken in the 1930s, and it was in 1938 that the centenary of the firm was celebrated. A special display was put on, covering 11 windows, of the changing fashion scene for ladies. A succession of plaster models displayed the poke bonnets of 1838; the bustles of 1868; the feathered hats, wasp waists and muffs of 1892; the pochettes, pot hats and pale pink stockings of 1926. The ladies were still holding pride of place, 43 years on from Charles Jenner's caryatids.

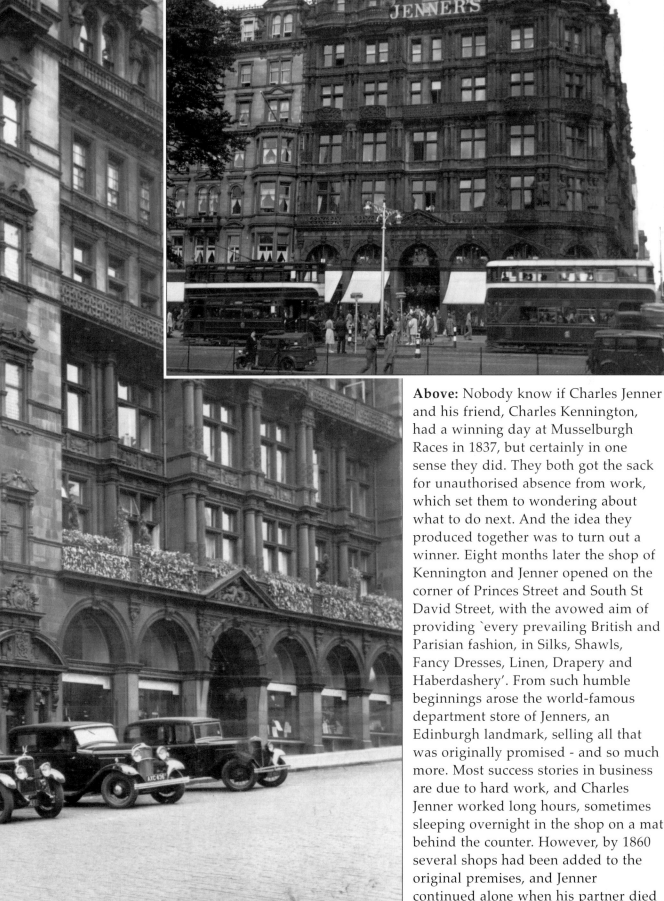

**Above:** Nobody know if Charles Jenner and his friend, Charles Kennington, had a winning day at Musselburgh Races in 1837, but certainly in one sense they did. They both got the sack for unauthorised absence from work, which set them to wondering about what to do next. And the idea they produced together was to turn out a winner. Eight months later the shop of Kennington and Jenner opened on the corner of Princes Street and South St David Street, with the avowed aim of providing `every prevailing British and Parisian fashion, in Silks, Shawls, Fancy Dresses, Linen, Drapery and Haberdashery'. From such humble beginnings arose the world-famous department store of Jenners, an Edinburgh landmark, selling all that was originally promised - and so much more. Most success stories in business are due to hard work, and Charles Jenner worked long hours, sometimes sleeping overnight in the shop on a mat behind the counter. However, by 1860 several shops had been added to the original premises, and Jenner continued alone when his partner died in 1863. This photograph of Jenners in the 1950s contains a nostalgic note in the shape of Edinburgh's wonderful old trams, which were gone by 1956.

**Above:** The photographer has caught a quiet time for this shot of Jenners, in the 1950s. It seems positively peaceful as shoppers browse amongst the socks and stockings, although the staff are busy enough with fabrics on the counter at bottom left. Towards the rear the sign for `Silk Stockings' seems to have a ring of the past about it, and even more so the pre-decimal price tag of 4/11d (25p.) Upstairs the china department, for the moment, is empty. After the first Jenners store had been destroyed by fire, in 1892, no expense was spared to create a truly magnificent replacement, which opened in 1895. The first consideration was a practical one - to make the building as fireproof as possible, hence a framework of iron columns and steel beams. After that, the interior décor was based on good taste and style, something of which can be seen in the carved oak of the upper gallery. Such features alone make Jenners a tourist attraction, but the store has always catered too for generations of Edinburgh family shoppers. Also it is a family firm in that the present chairman, Mr R D Miller, is the great-grandson of James Kennedy, who joined the firm in 1857.

**Above right:** Little did anyone know what a world of social change lay within this simple but elegant room at Jenners in the 1950s. The television age was dawning and nobody knew how it would transform our lives. There were those who thought it would be a passing fad (like rock `n' roll) and others who thought it would destroy civilisation. The expense of televisions made them a status symbol at first, and most people who watched the Coronation in 1953 will remember communal viewing in a school or a church hall. This made people want them, but the quality of the old black-and-white pictures was such that viewing invariably went on with lights out and curtains drawn. It was either BBC or the `off' switch, but many people will find those first television stars and programmes indelibly printed on their minds - `What's My Line?' with Gilbert Harding; Cliff Michelmore and `Tonight'; `Sunday Night at the London Palladium.' And, of course, it was felt that people couldn't possibly watch for too long without an `Interlude.' Wasn't that potter's wheel fascinating? Speaking of social change, the ash trays next to the viewing chairs at Jenners reveal a very different attitude towards smoking too in the 1950s.

**Below:** Gloves to the left; blouses, scarves and lace shawls to the right; all in elegant surroundings, with plenty of chairs for customers to sample the wares in comfort. This 1950s view from the entrance to the stairs shows some of the features which made Jenners a famous name in the world of department stores. Everything speaks of good taste, from the mosaic floor, through the panelling of the counters, to the decorative lights. Naturally the Jenners of today is not the same as the store of the 50s; change and development are part of progress. The former team of fitters were down to a mere two by 1985, and traditionalists were horrified at the vulgar idea of self-service in some of Jenners restaurants, along with a self-service coffee bar. In spite of a certain

amount of `streamlining,' there has been a constant widening of choice. A beauty salon, for example, was added in the 1980s. The store's argument is that in one sense Jenners remains as it has always been, a place with something for everyone, from mink coats to writing pads.

**Bottom:** This shot, again from the 1950s, is the previous Jenners picture in reverse, this time from the staircase to the entrance door of the oak-raftered, top-lit saloon. It gives a better chance to admire the fine carved oak woodwork of the staircase and gallery. The items for sale are, as before, gloves and neckwear at the far end. At the near end, to the left, we find purses, coathangers and travel accessories.

The picture was probably taken at a later date than the first, for more modern `Gloves' and `Neckwear' signs have appeared, and there are certainly fewer chairs. If the scene suggests serenity and calm, it has to be admitted that the store has had its moments of high drama. In 1984 an Edinburgh man attacked the perfume counters with a crowbar, and in the same year a fire-bomb was planted beneath a sofa in the furniture department. Both incidents were related to animal rights activists. Nevertheless, on the Queen's visit in 1988, on the 150th anniversary of Jenners, the stress was on stability as she spoke to Miss May Jeffrey, an employee in the silverware department for 42 years.

# At work

St Giles has witnessed any number of disturbances in its 500 year history, including the fiery preaching of John Knox, the stool throwing of Jenny Geddes in 1637 and, more recently, Hogmanay revelling outside its doors. It even suffered the indignity of having its statue of St Giles hurled into Nor' Loch during the sixteenth century Reformation. In the light of all this, perhaps a trade union gathering outside its doors was `small beer,' but it was important enough to those whom it involved in 1946. The immediate post-war years were ones of continued hardship. Workers found it difficult to keep up their living standards, and after six years of self-sacrifice during the war, they were not prepared to tolerate cost-cutting exercises at their expense. The building workers shown here outside St Giles were reacting angrily at the decision of their employers to end the official morning tea-break. The strike was official in that it had the support of the Amalgamated Union of Building Trade Workers, whose impressive banner can be seen to the rear. The trade union arguments were not just negative. `The Tea-Break Helps Production,' is the claim on one of the placards. Would anyone now disagree?

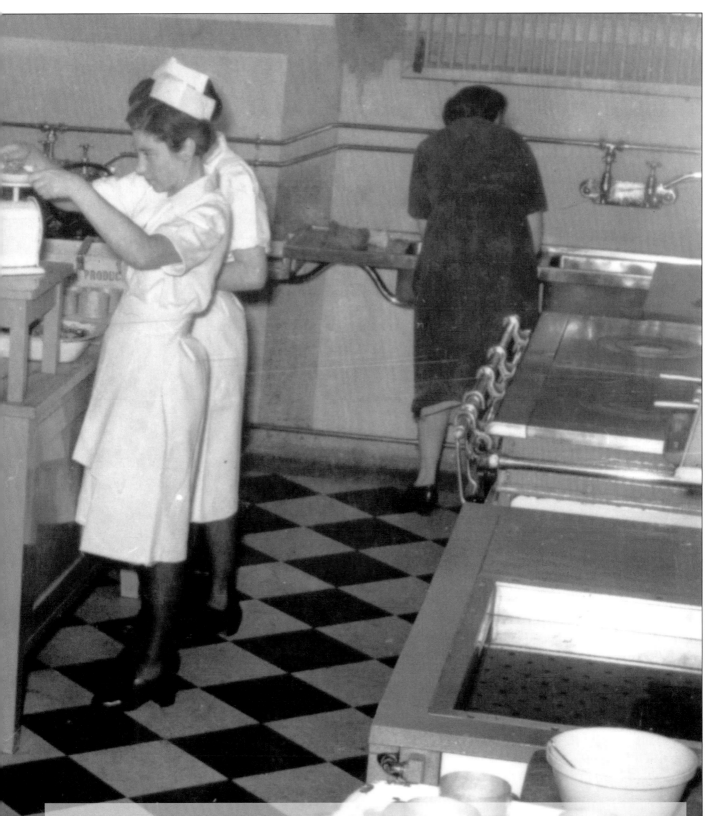

The cramped conditions in the Dietetics Kitchen of the Royal Infirmary of Edinburgh, in 1950, show a picture that had hardly changed since the opening of the kitchen, in 1928. Insulin for the treatment of diabetes, along with the scientific regulation of diet, were introduced into the Royal Infirmary in 1923. Edinburgh grew into one of the foremost diabetic treatment centres in the country, and the featured kitchen began its life as a Diabetic Kitchen. The problems facing some patients on their return home, in terms of continuing to take measured intakes of the correct foods, were tackled by the infirmary almoner and the associated Samaritans Society. For some patients it was the problem of a disciplined diet regime; for others it was simply the cost of buying the scales and the right food. The Diabetic Kitchen was opened to serve two research wards, a total of 12 beds, in 1928. However, it was soon called upon to provide special meals for many more patients with special dietary requirements, perhaps 40 to 50 daily. By 1938 Professor Dunlop was speaking of `chaos in the kitchen at mealtimes,' and a more spacious, up-to-date kitchen was opened but not until 1966.

Civil Defence took on enormous importance in World War II. In 1936 the Prime Minister of the day, Stanley Baldwin, had prophesied that `the bomber will always get through.' This turned out to be not quite the case, but in 1939 a great many civilian casualties, along with disruption of services, were expected from German bombing. Therefore civilians were urged to join some arm of Civil Defence. Many Edinburgh men joined the Local Defence Volunteers, or Home Guard, with the duty of defending an area stretching from Cramond Bridge to Wallyford Cross Roads,

**EDINBURGH HAD NO FEWER THAN 7,000 AIR-RAID WARDENS BY 1940**

including part of the Pentland Hills. More directly related to bombing, Edinburgh had no fewer than 7000 Air-Raid Wardens by 1940. Another vital unit was the Auxiliary Fire Service, the subject of the photograph. Mr David Adamson stands with his hand on the bonnet of the fine old truck, with its trailer of hoses attached. The picture was taken outside the Holy Cross School, which served as a temporary fire station. The equipment may not look much by modern standards, but the crew were trained, eager and ready for anything.

# An electrifying quality of service

John G Mackintosh have given top quality service in the electrical field since 1906 when electricity was both new and unusual. The founder set up a small works in South St David Street where the company remained for fifty eight years. J G Mackintosh sold out to Jack Reid in 1938 when steel conduit and wire fuses were still the norm.

Jack Reid was one of those unassuming pioneers who made history. During World War II he was directed into vital war work as an electrical researcher. His team was responsible for developing the ingenious 'De-gaussing' device which de-magnetised ships' metal hulls. This rendered both war ships and merchantmen safe from magnetic mines which previously had homed in on both friend and foe. Mr Reid received the MBE for 'services rendered'.

Since then although the expanding company has changed both premises and owners more than once it has maintained its A1 reputation. The present works are at 20/22 Nelson Street. Part of its success rests on the abilities and loyalty of long term employees who have worked for the partnership for thirty years or more.

The physical materials have altered to include PVC cables, alarms, switch gear and lighting systems undreamt of by the founder. The present customer base, in the industrial and commercial field, includes clients as well known as GEC Marconi, respected electrical pioneers themselves, Drambuie, British Gas and Jenners, one of Edinburgh's best loved stores.

J G Mackintosh enjoys the same long term working relationship with their clients as with their employees. It is doubly reassuring for a customer to rely on work being done by the same electrician. In these days of high risk security it is an additional benefit to know that regular maintenance work is done by qualified employees who are familiar with the electrical geography of a client's equipment. Add to this the knowledge that visiting employees have a spirit of customer loyalty only found amongst firms with a high regard for service and reputation.

*Below: Bill Brown (left) and Jimmy Dick.*

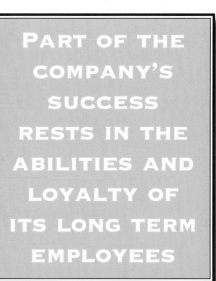

PART OF THE COMPANY'S SUCCESS RESTS IN THE ABILITIES AND LOYALTY OF ITS LONG TERM EMPLOYEES

# *From cockpen to palace and yacht*

The Edinburgh designers, furnishers and restorers Whytock and Reid were amalgamated in 1875 by the combination of two successful firms founded earlier in the nineteenth century. Since then they have gone from strength to strength, certain in the knowledge of a market for the best in quality of design, workmanship and materials.

Richard Whytock established his business in 1807 in the heyday of the intermittant but deliciously extravagant Regency period. In the same year the 'Corsican Ogre', Napoleon, signed the short lived Treaty of Tilsit with Czar Alexander to cement peaceful relations between the vast primitive Empire of All the Russias and the all-conquering Empire of the French. The latter was to be brought to its knees in eight years' time thanks, in part, to the Duke of Wellington's hard-fighting Highland regiments and largely to Britain's wealth and naval and manufacturing superiority.

*Above right:* An invoice dating from August 1909.
*Below:* The workshop circa 1920.

The 'auld alliance' between the Scots and the French was 'lang syne deid' as Britain was in the throes of a twenty-five year long war with France largely financed by the fast-developing wealth of the Industrial Revolution. The pioneering agricultural work of the Lowland Improvers was being matched

by that of Scots inventors, engineers and mill owners throughout both Scotland's ancient trading cities and the new industrial settlements of the Lowlands. The heavyweight naval gun, nicknamed 'the Smasher', was produced in the Carron Iron Works after which it was named the carronade.

It was in these tumultuous decades that those who aspired by virtue of birth, or by their own ingenuity and efforts, to membership of good society throughout fashionable centres, such as 'Auld Reekie's' famous Adamesque New Town, called upon the services of cabinetmakers, upholsterers and carpet weavers such as Richard Whytock.
Here, as in Pre-Revolutionary France, the fashionable world's insatiable demands for the latest styles in clothing, household decorations, furniture, fabrics and carriages et al reflected the 'modus vivendi' of the wealthy throughout the entire civilised world.

the customers their wealth also provided the young Richard Whytock with the impetus to found a threefold manufactory to cater both for the inhabitants of Edinburgh and for the landowners, who not only had town houses in Scotland's capital but who also desired that their country seats be furnished in the most up-to-date styles.

His son carried on in the family tradition of working with locally-produced hardwoods such as oak, beech and elm, which could be brought in by horse drawn wagons. Tropical hardwoods, such as mahogany, teak and satinwood, were shipped home from the Indies at a time when Malay pirates, following the days of French privateers, added to the financial risks of keeping ahead of competitors. Eventually, in 1875 he went into partnership with the similar firm founded by John Reid in 1820.

On Scotland's west coast, in 1820, John Reid, a time served upholstery apprentice turned journeyman craftsman, had set up his workshop at 26 Sandgate in Ayr. His seven year apprenticeship had cost his parents £100 Scots, a small fortune in the early years of the nineteenth century, only put together by sacrifices on the part of his parents. By 1851, the year of the Great Exhibition at the Crystal Palace in London, John Reid was employing fifteen journeymen and seven boys. They too worked, as did all cabinetmakers and upholsterers of the period, using the same materials, tools and skills employed in the Whytock workshops.

It was this ever-changing demand which provided employment for regiments of skilled craftsmen and women working to the highest standards in their fields. Despite the uncertainties of wartime, such a client base was little affected, although they grumbled at the iniquitous rise of Income Tax to the unheard of level of 1/7d (8p) in the pound! The atmosphere of expansion which gave

*Above: Two Cockpen chairs produced by the company.*
*Right: Belford Cabinet Works.*

French style with the guid Scots craftmanship and solidity of build desired by customers of the burgeoning middle classes who, above all, wanted their homes to appear respectable. The French lawn game of Croquet had become acceptable but Tennis was initially regarded as being racy and as suspect as a jolly French Sunday. Obviously, combining such diverse national characteristics in furniture and decoration fashions was a marketing minefield which called for discretion as much as verve.

What became known as the Whytock and Reid Style was fully developed by a partnership between Murray Reid, Hugh's son, and the designer William Simpson with the designer-carver John Murray. From the 1890s to the 1930s the trio were responsible for overseeing an era of superb craftsmanship coupled with a typically Scots blend of 'inventive traditionalism'. They frequently worked hand in glove with the famous Scots architect Sir Robert Lorimer in designing well-matched house interiors and furnishings for commissions in what became well known Scottish houses such as Earlshall, Hill of

Alive to the latest demands for French styles, he sent his sons, Hugh, Robert and David, to 'ateliers', which are design studios and workshops, in the booming Paris of the Second Empire. This was founded in 1852 by Napoleon's grandson, President turned Emperor Napoleon III. He stimulated the rebuilding of the city and a rebirth of Parisian taste and fashion, led by Empress Eugenie of part Scots, part-Spanish parentage, and catered for by Worth, an English dress designer whose styles spread throughout Europe and the civilised parts of Russia and the Americas.

Tarvit, Kellie and Marchmont and others of that ilk. Imagine the joy of being able to afford such a partnership of genius in building and furnishing one's home.

*Above: A weather vane restored by the company.*
*Below: Chair manufacture.*

The three boys returned home inspired by their educational training experience in the exciting and elegant capital of a Catholic and Latinesque nation, so different from life in Victorian Scotland dominated by the puritanical canons of the Presbyterian churches. They succeeded in marrying the vivacity of

Sir Robert was a frequent visitor to the company's workshops in Belford Mews where his sketches were translated into scale drawings and from them into works of art.

Murray Reid encouraged innovations in all the decorative arts, including the famous 'musical stripes' pattern fabric designed and woven by Mr McBride in the west for use as furnishing and curtain material. His daughter Hope Mullens recalls how these vivid, beautiful and hard-wearing fabrics flitted from house to house whenever the Reids moved. Being a thrifty family, the girls often wore dresses made of curtain fabrics which caused Hope and her sister, as school girls, some embarrassment when visiting one of many private steam yachts outfitted by Whytock and Reid, to find that their dresses matched the saloon curtains!

She recalls a happier occasion when Queen Mary visited the works to inspect a bedroom suite ordered for the Holyrood Palace rooms of her younger son, the then Duke of York who became King George VI, father of our present Queen. As the Reids were on holiday in Arran Hope's father returned to Edinburgh to host HM, who asked of the tropical woods 'Are all these woods British?'. In those days everyone believed 'British was Best' and bought nothing else, even if the raw materials were from the Empire.

In 1934 Murray Reid sold the George Street premises and moved to 7 Charlotte Square where the firm's showrooms stayed until 1973, when the National Trust for Scotland aquired the property now known as the Georgian

House. Appropriately enough this beautiful building was refurbished with the help of Whytock and Reid who have had the pleasure of refurbishing a number of NTS properties including Haddo House and both Brodie and Culzean Castles.

Other prestigious private and commercial clients from amongst those for whom only the best will do include banks, breweries and other businesses where the boardrooms, entrance halls and executive offices reflect the taste and wealth of the customer. One of the company's most recent jobs was assisting with the refurbishment of the private apartments on the former Royal Yacht Britannia. In 1964 David Reid joined his father, Campbell, and ten years later moved the showrooms from the elegance of Charlotte Square to newly-built Sunbury House by the quiet beauty of the Water of Leith. Campbell Reid's enthusiasm for hand-woven textiles extended from the traditional oriental pieces, which are such a sound investment, to his own innovative designs woven in Portuguese studios.

In 1994 David Reid became the fifth generation to hold the Royal Warrant first granted in 1838. The firm's stock includes antiques as well as many pieces made throughout its history, all of which are for those clients, whether corporate or private, who appreciate the finest quality and style.

*Above: Another stage in the manufacturing process.*
*Below: The company's premises at Belford Mews.*

# SCA Packaging Ltd

Children are fascinated by corrugated cardboard as they wonder how the crinkly inner layer was sandwiched between the two flat layers of this immensely strong form of cardboard. Whisky distillers and medicine manufacturers alike entrust their precious products, in breakable glass bottles, to corrugated board cases for transit to distant destinations. Equally heavy packs of butter and easily bruised fruit also cross international boundaries protected by the miracle board which has been produced in Edinburgh for over sixty years.

The earliest paper making is credited to both the Chinese and the Ancient Egyptians. The British used sheepskin parchment for centuries until the first British paper mill was established in Hertfordshire in 1490, close enough to supply William Caxton's revolutionary printing works in London. The early papers, and even modern handmade papers, were and are made of fibrous plant materials such as nettles, straw and flax. Mass produced papers and boards rely on constant supplies of wood chips, straw and recycled paper and board.

An early form of paper laminated with strawboard was in use for packaging before 1850. The first use of corrugated paper in England was for the corrugated hatbands patented in 1856 by Healey and Allen. The first corrugated packaging was patented in the USA only a few years before Thompson and Norris started production in Britain in 1883.

By the early 1930s the Thompson & Norris Manufacturing Company Ltd of 248 Easter Road, Edinburgh with factories in Acton, Brentford, Histon and far off Durban in the Union of South Africa needed to expand. The company chose a green fields site on the outskirts of 'Auld Reekie', at what became Number 1 Turnhouse Road, for their new Scottish works. The total cost of building the plant came to £60,000 at a time when many families lived on a few pounds a week and top managers on £500 a year were considered wealthy.

The roadside frontage decorated in the striking Art Deco style of the period is now a listed building while the factory was fitted with the most up to date plant for turning reels of paper into corrugated board.

The majority of the pre-war customers were the independent bakers and canners whose once well loved and trusted trade marks have been swallowed

***Below and facing page:*** *The factory being built in 1934.*

up by great monopolies. School children spent their pennies on bags of broken biscuits from the bottom of the biscuit tins in which loose biscuits were carefully packed while their mothers bought canned foods which were delivered to the shops in corrugated board boxes until the 1970s.

Many readers will remember the sturdy partitioned wooden boxes in which wines, spirits and bottled beers rattled about on horse drawn drays and motor lorries until such boxes were replaced by board and plastic. Eggs too, on the familiar board trays of thirty, were transported in wooden crates until these gave way to corrugated board.

> THE EDINBURGH FACTORY WAS AT ONE TIME THE BIGGEST CUSTOMER FOR THE EAST OF SCOTLAND REGION OF BRITISH RAILWAYS

Long distance journeys to and from the factory went by train as a matter of course. The railway companies took total responsibility for collecting and delivering using their own horse drawn and motor vehicles for the shorter hauls to and from their goods yards or branch line stations. A later post-war development was the interchangeable rail-road container which reduced manhandling to a minimum.

And people say integrated transport systems are new! The Edinburgh factory was at one time the biggest customer for the East of Scotland region of the nationalised British Railways. Today everything goes by road.

So great was the output of the Edinburgh factory that it supplied customers throughout Scotland and Northern England until new works were built in the 1950s and 60s in Wigan, near the one time inland port of Manchester, and at Hartlepool on the north-east coast. Demand was rising not only from the traditional clients of the food packaging industry but also from the gradual conversion of spirits, beer and eggs from wood to corrugated and in the expanding areas of household appliances and electronics. Insatiable public buying of kitchen equipment and TVs, radiograms and power tools not to mention flat pack DIY furniture kits and home computers led to enhanced purchasing of corrugated board by all manufacturers of these items. Some 70% of all retail goods sold in Britain are packed in corrugated board. Those who concern themselves with the

environmental friendly disposal of packaging materials will be pleased to note that the food and drinks industry alone recovers 82% of its corrugated board containers. Modern corrugated board contains up to 70% recycled fibre thanks to legislation fixing responsibility for its disposal onto the manufacturer and retailer. Stable owners are turning to recycled shredded corrugated board as a viable alternative to straw for horse bedding.

Supermarket customers who prefer to put their shopping into boxes rather than in floppy plastic bags can always add the board to their compost heaps. Much of the new paper used in the board industry comes from properly farmed forests where felled trees are replaced by planted young stock along the traditional lines of good husbandry

*Above: Some of the many uses for the company's product.*

mooted by organisations such as the Forest Stewardship Scheme.

Corrugated cardboard consists of three layers of paper glued together in a wavy centred sandwich. Three enormous reels of paper are fed simultaneously through a board making machine not unlike a huge textile, linoleum or newsprint printing press. The centre layer is corrugated by being passed through rollers rather like a giant version of the Victorian crimping rollers. This and the two flat outer layers of the paper sandwich are glued together to form very strong board of varying thicknesses.

The next processes consist of slotting and creasing the made up board to required sizes. The manufacturer can also print brand names, contents type and numbers and handling instructions in up to four colours and in any language to suit the customers and their intended markets To save space in transit and storage the containers are delivered flat to the clients' premises. It is for this reason that retailers also undo and pack together flattened boxes for collection by waste collectors.

The volumes attained by production lines in any industry today are so considerable that even a single line can fill between ten and twenty thousand cases a day! It follows that box manufacturers such as the SCA Packaging plant at Turnhouse Road have to maintain reliable deliveries to customers who do not

wish to tie up space and money in large stocks of boxes. During the history of board production at this site each of the five firms involved, namely Thomson and Norris, then Albert E Reed, which was superseded by Reed Corrugated Cases which gave way to Reedpack until taken over by the Swedish firm SCA, have upgraded and replaced the machinery as new machines are tested and produced in order to keep up with the continually growing world-wide demand.

Other factors have also changed with the times. There was once so much manual and clerical work involved that 560 people, of whom 40% were women, worked here. Dayshift workers were served by a small fleet of five buses which ferried the workers between their homes in outlying villages and the factory. Today the highly automated works employs 190 with the ladies working, in the main, in the offices. Even the 20-30 students, who for generations came here in the summer to cover for staff on holiday, are redundant because modern machinery and handling processes are now largely automated. The latest board making

machines can run at speeds of over 200 metres, nearly 220 yards, of board per minute, that is over 13,000 yards or nearly fifteen miles an hour. For the youngsters who use the metric system that equals some 50,000 linear kilometres of board per annum.

In line with the modernisation of processes are the new machines which can cope with printing and closing in one continuous operation. This saves the considerable time and effort involved in moving and setting into position the enormous volumes of immensely heavy and cumbersome materials.

UK output is used by the Food and Drink processing industries which take 44%, Scientific Instruments, Clocks, Photographic and Optical goods account for 15%. Farmers and Growers take 10% of UK corrugated board while Electrical and Electronic goods use 7% of output. Soaps, Perfumes and Cosmetics use 6% leaving 18% to be used by other miscellaneous producers.

*Above: The Reed factory in 1967.*

# William Hunter: the company that has paid attention for almost 120 years

William Hunter began his coal haulage business in 1880 at Lamb's place, Loanhead, originally using just one horse and cart to haul coal between the various mining villages in Midlothian. This was back-breaking work, and provided little light relief, so at weekends William ventured into a more glamorous business, providing horses and traps for weddings and outings.

The little business grew quickly with the passenger side of the business coming to the fore. At the turn of the century it moved to larger premises just a quarter of a mile down the road.

The first world war obviously held expansion back but the company quickly recovered to such an extent that by the 1920s the company was able to invest in its first motor vehicles and charabancs.

The distinctive brown and cream livery of the fleet is regularly seen in all corners of the UK and Europe, and a wide cross section of society including local government, schools, tour companies and universities take advantage of the reasonable prices and first class service.

In almost 120 years of trading in Edinburgh, Hunter's Coaches has maintained the integral part of its business and its motto 'We pay attention' is as true today as it ever was.

Many a local Scout or Guide was transported to camp or on the annual school trip.

By the 1950s the company had decided to concentrate solely on passenger transport using the most up-to-date vehicles of the time.

It was a move which was to prove fortunate. Since that time the company has become renowned for its attention to every detail and the comfort it offers its passengers.

*Above:* An early boy scout trip.
*Facing page, top right:* An early soft top chara with George Hunter stood beside it.
*Facing page, top left:* William Hunter, founder of the company.
*Facing page, bottom:* The original horse and cart dating from c1920.
*Below:* Part of Hunters' modern fleet.

# Quality, service and reliability for over forty years

Richard Malone opened a bakery at 40 Ashley Terrace in November 1953. Dick Malone, as he was known by the locals, was a time served baker with Edinburgh & Dumfrishshire Dairy Company Limited. These were his first premises and he provided rolls, bran scones, butteries and confectionery for both the retail and wholesale markets. Dick originally did all the baking and delivering himself.

In August 1962 Dick moved premises to one shop - 115 Slateford Road. This was primarily because of the complaints he had been receiving from other tenants about the noise of the bakery machinery on a Saturday night - as well as feeling that the unusual market of selling rolls in the evening through until early morning would be better off at Slateford Road. This proved to be correct and Dick then proceeded to buy the shop next door in July 1963 - 113 Slateford Road. When Dick moved to Slateford Road all confectionery products were stopped and he concentrated on White Morning Rolls, Bran Scones and Butteries only. The bakery premises had an oven, one small dough mixing machine and two proving machines. The bakery then gradually expanded whereby three full-time bakers

were taken on as well as there being two delivery vans on the road. From around 1968 Dick Malone retired from the baking side of the business.

The business was sold to an outsider in 1974 and in 1975 Sylvia Mason became a partner for a three year period until 1978 when she became sole proprietrix of R & J Malone's Bakeries, the name by which it is still known. Ms Mason has kept the premises the same in that 115 Slateford Road is still the original bake-house and 113 Slateford Road is still the retail shop.

It was not until 1978 that the business really began to expand from just 3 roll products to gradually over 20 different kinds of roll products sold today, as well as the expansion of the retail shop into a Take-Away shop. Ms Mason created the logo of "quality, service and reliability " and has upgraded the bakery according to these standards, over the years, using her selling and business experience. Malone's Bakeries has never changed its trait of its unusual opening hours to the retail customer and is still known for opening from 8pm until 3am to purchase fresh rolls. It is open 361 days a year, seven days a week, only closing for two days at Christmas and New Year respectively. Wholesale products make up the main proportion of the business and two delivery vans are still used, although the vans are now much larger.

In November 1989 a national flour mill commended Malone's for excellence in the production of its Scottish Morning Rolls.

Ms Mason's daughter joined the business in a full-time capacity in 1994 to direct and advise in the

computing and administration areas of the business, thereby relieving Ms Mason of more time to market Malone's products. This then led to the planning of what was to be the largest of all refurbishments which took place in September 1995 over two weeks. The bakery was closed for the first time in over 33 years, for more than two days. Old floors were replaced, machinery was completely revamped and a new gas oven replaced the old deck ovens and the retail shop was upgraded.

Not much has changed over the years with regards to raw materials and equipment. Although a different, but unique recipe is now used for the morning rolls, the bran scone recipe has never changed. The Aberdeen buttery roll recipe was started in the late 60s by an Aberdonian baker but the recipe had to be modified to take out a proportion of the salt as the locals did not like it and to this day it remains the same recipe but is now known as a buttery, without the Aberdeen part, being the extra salt flavour.

*Above:* R & J Malone were awarded this certificate for their Morning Rolls in October 1989.
*Left:* One of the company's vans from the early 1990s.
*Below:* This photograph dates from the 1980s and shows one of the original ovens which were used until 1995.

# The family firm that has carved its niche in Edinburgh

The joinery firm of George Hardie and Son is believed to have been founded in 1882, although it could be claimed that its earliest contribution to the building of Edinburgh dates back to more than 130 years ago, when George Hardie himself worked on the building of the General Post Office. The foundation stone for the GPO was laid in 1861, and the building was completed in 1866. George Hardie is thought to have come from Melrose. He was living at 4 Little King Street in 1866, and remained in Edinburgh, going on to establish the joinery firm whose work can be seen throughout the city, and whose many contracts were to include the building of the janitors' houses at Moray House Training College in 1907, and the construction of houses in Ravelston Dykes and Greenend in 1934 in conjunction with other firms who combined to form the Edinburgh Building Company. George's son John was to make teak fronts for all the Rutherford Bars around 1920, of which two still remain, one being The Iron Duke at the top of Leith Street. The firm was also responsible for the front elevation of the Edinburgh Savings Bank, where the wood carving was done by Mr Good; for Mackies Butteries in Princes Street, where stained silver birch treated in Holland was used; and for all the windows and half the joinery work at New City Chambers.

However, after the completion of the GPO George Hardie's next employment was with James Doull and Co, who had a workshop at 6 Park Street. When James Doull died, George Hardie carried on the business as foreman, eventually purchasing it from Mrs Doull. Records show that George Hardie paid £5-0s-0d to the Doull Trust in 1882 in respect of a half-year's rent for the workshop.

Mr Hardie's last rent on 6 Park Street was paid in 1894, after which time the building was demolished to make way for the McEwan Hall and the workshop was moved to premises on Candlemaker Row which had formerly been occupied by McAndrew Builders.

*Below: A family portrait with George Hardie in the centre.*

There they sold ironmongery and small pieces of timber, small bags of coal, and paraffin from a huge tank which was there when they bought the shop. In 1973 the firm closed the shop and turned 9 Colinton Road into its offices.

John's death in 1963 left Frederick as sole partner in the business. In 1965 he bought William Skinner's builders business at 36-38 Potterrow. The accommodation here was superior to that at Belford Road, and so Belford Road was rented out and later sold. George Hardie and Son has remained at 36-38 Potterrow ever since, although another move is envisaged in the near future. Frederick retired in August 1983 and the firm is now run by his three sons, John who is Managing Director, David who is a Director and Graeme who still works as a joiner and assists with the running of the business.

George Hardie's have also worked on several historic buildings over the last thirty years, in many churches around Edinburgh, and at Winton House in Pencaitland, where extensive dry rot eradication was carried out over a period of several years.

*Above: Joiners at the Chapel Street Workshop in 1890.*
*Below: A later view of the company's premises.*

One problem encountered at Candlemaker Row was the 'Gardyloo' - the rubbish thrown into the yard - and the business moved from here to 18 Chapel Street, formerly the premises of Paterson, Blindmaker, where it stayed until 1956. Here, the house became the family residence and there was a two-storey workshop, usually ankle-deep in sawdust and shavings, in the garden and an office, which until 1948 had gas lighting and an old gas radiator which gave off appalling fumes, in the old hen house.

The firm is first referred to as George Hardie and Sons in 1898. George's sons were James, George and John. James, the eldest, was the only one who did not train as a joiner; George and John both worked with their father.

After George's death in 1903 James took over the business with John as foreman. John became a partner in 1926, and finally took over, with his younger son Frederick, when James retired in 1948. In 1956 John and Fred bought new premises at 14 Belford Road. This was an old mill which had been converted and now had workshops on three storeys, and cost £600; the premises were not ideal, as for one thing carrying long lengths of wood into the workshops was difficult, and the business remained there for less than ten years. John and Fred also opened a 'Do-It-Yourself' shop at 9 Colinton Road in 1963.

# 120 years of food equipment and machinery

Supplying specialist tools to the Baking industry for nearly 120 years, and the Hospitality and Catering industry for 50, Scobie & McIntosh hold something of a record, and their name has become synonymous with quality and friendly service over that time.

It all started over 120 years ago when Mr Scobie and Mr McIntosh formed the original company. Mr Scobie did not remain and left Mr McIntosh to start the family interest which continues today. The early beginnings included manufacture of baking tins for bread, alongside a myriad of hand tools with forgotten names, like Dockers, Peels, Hozzles and Chains, and Fomenting Tubs. The Company's catalogue of 1904 makes fascinating reading.

Housed at first in Niddrie Street in Edinburgh, it moved to 53 Cockburn Street with a Works at Greenside Place (behind the Playhouse Theatre). The product range widened to include ornate copper tea and coffee urns and early machinery for bakers.

*Right, both pictures: Two images of the Works in 1904. The pictures originate from a company brochure.*

Memories of one of the works staff who retired in 1978 after 56 years with the company were as a boy of 14 making deliveries around Edinburgh by horse and cart. He with three colleagues served over 200 years with the Company.

It is interesting to note that the works made vanes for Aerial Torpedoes in the Great War and casings for Marine radios in the second world war.

In 1922 the Company under the last Mr McIntosh or 'Uncle Mac' as he was affectionately known,

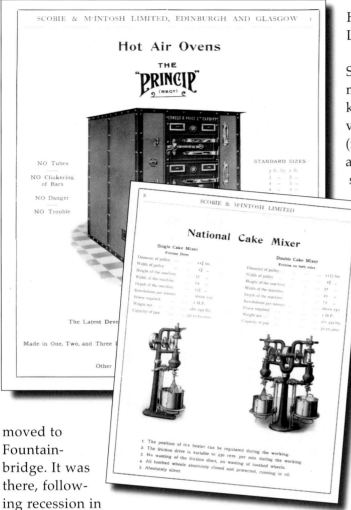

Holland, Austria and the USA, and led by Prue Leith and Willie Rushton.

Self-service food display counters became the main production and are seen in major supermarkets today. Kitchen installations became extremely varied, and clients included Football Stadia (notably Rangers, Celtic, Hearts, Hibs, Aberdeen and many English clubs), oil rig galleys, hotels, schools and hospital kitchens. The emerging supermarket bakeries became customers alongside the craft bakers.

To focus on these distinctly different markets, the company was divided into two separate trading entities. Scobie & McIntosh (Catering Equipment) Ltd led by a Buy-in team is located today in Livingston. Scobie & McIntosh (Bakery Engineers) Ltd, still the original family business is now at Minto Street, Edinburgh, with a test bakery and engineering teams in Leeds. It has become a leading supplier of machinery and plant for the Food Processing and Baking industries.

The current Chairman's son Timothy continues the family tradition of innovation, running his own design house - Food Service Partnership Ltd - providing a design and management service based on state of the art Computer Design facilities.

*Above: Two pages from the company's 1926 brochure. Below: Prue Leith at the International Catering Conference in 1988.*

moved to Fountainbridge. It was there, following recession in the 30s, that the company was taken under the wing of Uncle Mac's brothers-in-law, James and John Brown, Ironfounders and owners of Forth and Clyde and Sunniside Ironworks in Falkirk. James, a strong and staunchly patriotic Scot, determined his daughter should not marry her true love, a Sassenach, was sure he could prevent the match by insisting the dowry should be the small loss-making company. He did not reckon on the determination of Peter Alderson who took up the challenge, giving up a career in law in London to do so. He gradually changed the image of the Company into a respected national supplier, and introduced, with great vision, Catering equipment in the early 50s. The factory moved to Annandale Street and began production of stainless steel fabrications. Branches were then in Aberdeen, Glasgow, Belfast and Newcastle.

His son Geoffrey Alderson joined the company in 1965 and was despatched South to develop the English end of the market, returning to Edinburgh in 1978 to take over the reins.

The Company moved to Sighthill in 1988, opening the new factory and showroom with a major international Conference including key speakers from

# A taste of Italy in the heart of Scotland

Ask anyone from Edinburgh where to find the finest ice-cream in the area and he will answer "Mr Boni's, of course". Mr Boni's has had a presence in Edinburgh since just after the first world war and was an enterprise began by an young Italian man who came to Scotland (as many had before him) at the turn of the century, to escape the poverty in the Frosinone area of Italy.

### Early days
Biagio Boni had already made a name for himself with a small venture in Gilmore Place called the Empress Café by the time he invited his younger brother, Guiseppe, over in 1910.

The café was an elegant affair with a pianola to keep the customers entertained and stained glass windows to add to the atmosphere. Although the business ticked over nicely the brothers weren't willing to just sit back and wait for custom to come their way.

*Below: One of the company's earliest motorised delivery vans with Joseph Boni kneeling down in the centre.*

Instead, they took to the streets with a hand barrow to sell their ice-cream to the population in the capital. From this small step followed a horse and cart which became a well-known and well loved sight in Edinburgh's beauty spots.

There followed a time of diversification, with Biagio eventually moving into the cones and wafers side of the ice-cream business and Guiseppe taking control of the café in 1932. Guiseppe remained there until his untimely death in 1945, after which his widow, Jennifer, stepped in, with their fifteen year old son, Lawrence, joining the venture two years later. They were difficult times and the family worked long hours to make the business work...and work it did. Lawrence can recall practically living at the café with all their meals being taken in the back shop. They had their fair share of regulars, one in particular that springs to his mind to this day, an elderly spinster who called in at the same time every day for coffee and a cigarette. She was always on hand to help Lawrence with his homework.

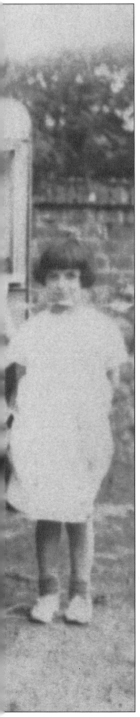

The Empress was closed in the 1960s to make way for the 'ultra-modern' Quernstone Restaurant. By this time, Lawrence had married and he and his wife, Anita, had three sons, Stefano, Ricardo and Josef, who although very young at the time, quickly learned to appreciate their very own ice-cream parlour. By the time the café underwent its third transformation, which took place in 1979, the brothers were old enough to become involved, helping out after school and during holidays.

Mr Boni's has the honour of being the first of its kind in Scotland and offered a huge range of flavours

even in its infancy. Lawrence, buoyed up by his success was able to import a 24 flavour unit during the 1970s from Italy.

Stefano, the oldest of his sons, meanwhile was studying hotel management with every intention of joining the family business at some stage. This honour was thrust upon him rather sooner than he had thought. Lawrence was elected as President of the Ice Cream Alliance which, he realised, would take up a lot of his time . Twenty one year old Stefano eagerly came aboard. Since that time the venture has grown with two of the three sons joining the business (Ricardo chose an alternative career).

Stefano describes ice-cream as really part of the entertainment industry. "After all," he says, "it's a fun business! Eating ice-cream makes everyone happy."

***Above:*** *Joseph Boni, founder of the company.*

> ICE CREAM IS REALLY PART OF THE ENTERTAINMENT INDUSTRY...AFTER ALL, IT'S A FUN BUSINESS! EATING ICE-CREAM MAKES EVERYONE HAPPY

# Made by Scotts for Scots - and shared with the rest of the world

There can be no name more Scottish than Scott, and nothing more Scottish than a sporran; so a sporran manufacturer called Scott and Son really must be about as Scottish as you can get!

Scotsmen used to wear sporrans to keep their oats, gunpowder and cash dry. After the 1745 rebellion sporrans were banned along with the rest of traditional dress, but when the kilt was reintroduced 200 years ago, sporrans came back too; after all, every true Scot needs somewhere safe to put his money.

When sadler William Scott started up in business in the 1930s, he was one of scores of sporran-makers throughout Scotland. The current proprietor, Malcolm Scott, grandson of William Scott, is one of less than half a dozen sporran-makers still in existence, and by far the biggest; more than half the craftsmen who work in the business are employed by him in his workshop in Causewayside and the firm probably makes more than three times as many sporrans as all the other manufacturers put together. The three generations of Scotts have made few changes to the workshop, so that it has retained a distinctly Dickensian feel, with its pre-war gas fires and ancient wooden benches. Here some 10,000 sporrans are made each year, in addition to other accessories such as waistbelts, chain straps, dress belts, cross belts, and special belts, drum slings and harnesses for pipe bands.

The busiest time of year for Malcolm Scott comes in the New Year, when preparations are being made for Burns suppers, and sporrans are in great demand. Malcolm supplies

**HIGH PROFILE SPORRAN WEARERS HAVE INCLUDED SIR ALEC GUINESS, ROGER MOORE AND MICHAEL CAINE**

most shops which sell or hire out Highland outfits, and offers a choice of more than 130 designs; there are small sporrans less than four inches across for children, sporrans for day wear, semi-dress sporrans which have some embellishments and can be used for day or evening wear, and full dress sporrans exclusively for evening wear. A good sporran will cost well into three figures, while those with expensive tastes might choose to spend £2,500 or more on a sporran highly decorated with silver.

High-profile sporran-wearers have included the Alexander Brothers and Kenneth McKellar, Sir Alec Guinness when he played Bonnie Prince Charlie,

he could turn it into a sporran. An examination of the skin and documentation provided established that the leopard died of old age many years ago and the skin had been kept in a cupboard for 30 years; this proved, Malcolm made one sporran out of it, which featured the leopard's head which had been stuffed by a taxidermist.

Most sporrans these days, it has to be said, are not as Scottish as they used to be in terms of the actual materials used in their manufacture; the metal 'findings' used as decoration partially come from Birmingham, leather might come from Brazil, Belgium or Argentina, horsehair comes from Paraguay and is processed in East Anglia, and it is cheaper to buy pigskin from Italy than from the UK. But sporrans are still made in the traditional way, with Scottish craftsmen and women stitching, glueing, trimming and tooling away busily in the old-fashioned workshop in Causewayside, keeping their countrymen, and the world, supplied with sporrans, and keeping one of Scotland's traditional craft industries very much alive.

Roger Moore, Michael Caine, and famous Scottish regiments such as the Black Watch, the Scots Guards and the Gordon Highlanders; all of them have chosen sporrans made by William E Scott and Son. But there can be no finer sight in kilt and sporran than Malcolm Scott himself, all twenty stone of him, plus beard and long hair.

A significant amount of William E Scott and Son's goods are exported, to the USA , Canada, New Zealand, Australia and South Africa, and also Italy, Germany, Holland and Sweden, where pipebands have become popular. From time to time the international fashion industry puts tartan and sporrans into the limelight; during the eighties, W E Scott shipped out a whole ton of sporrans to France where, worn as shoulder bags, they had become the latest Paris fashion, and exports soared again when Japanese ladies took to using sporrans as handbags.

Possibly the most unusual sporran which Malcolm Scott has ever made was for Chief Mangosuthu Buthelezi, leader of the Zulu Inkatha freedom movement in South Africa, as a gift to the King of the Zulus; Chief Buthelezi provided a leopard skin, and Malcolm Scott had to ascertain that the leopard had died of natural causes before

*Above: An age-old tradition in a modern-day surroundings.*
*Facing page: Malcolm Scott with the leopard's head sporran for Chief Buthelezi.*
*Below: Malcolm Scott outside his Edinburgh premises*

# You can't get better than a Kwik-Fit fitter

As car ownership has increased, so it has become more important for automotive specialists to recognise the changing needs of the motorist. In 1971 the automotive industry was transformed when Sir Tom Farmer CBE established Kwik-Fit. Specialising in the repair and replacement of the most common automotive parts, Kwik-Fit was founded on a very simple, but at the time, revolutionary idea - that the most important person in the organisation is the customer.

The first Kwik-Fit Centre opened in McDonald Road, Edinburgh and offered a 'drive in, while you wait' service. Since then, Kwik-Fit has developed a product range and expertise that covers motorists essential needs: tyres, exhausts, brakes, batteries, suspension, lubrication and in-car safety products. The Kwik-Fit Group now operates from almost 2,000 centres, Kwik-Fit Mobile tyre fitting vehicles, Tyre Plus Autoservice, Speedy and Pit-Stop centres in the UK, Eire, Holland, Belgium, Germany, France and

Spain. More than 10,000 people work for the Kwik-Fit Group which also includes Kwik-Fit Insurance Services, a telemarketing unit that sells Kwik-Fit branded motor policies on behalf of leading insurance underwriters.

*Above:* An early newspaper advertisement for Kwik-Fit.
*Below:* Kwik-Fit's Central Support office and adjacent Kwik-Fit centre at Murrayfield.

Kwik-Fit's aim is 100% customer delight. A culture of continuous improvement has created a fast, efficient and friendly experience backed by quality, choice and value for money. ISO 9002 backed systems help deliver the right product in the right place at the right time. Convenient, accessible and well presented centres, the Kwik-Fit Code of Practice and a continuous investment in training and development programmes also help Kwik-Fit people exceed customers' basic expectations.

Kwik-Fit people are supported and trained to be the best in the industry. Through Kwik-Fit's four training centres in the UK, Holland and France and a purpose built, high tech, multi-media Training Academy, Kwik-Fit people can work towards nationally recognised qualifications which complement Kwik-Fit's bespoke training programmes. In 1993, Kwik-Fit achieved the Investors in People standard and this has helped Kwik-Fit build on its established and

professional training programmes. Together with Kwik-Fit's structured career ladder, it means that all Kwik-Fit people have the same opportunity to progress and succeed.

Kwik-Fit depend on and value everything their people do. It is their enthusiasm and commitment to deliver a first class service that has helped to drive the business forward. In return, Kwik-Fit provides job security and a renumeration programme that includes a competitive basic salary and a share in the profits they help to create through profit related pay and an employee share scheme in which more than 2,000 people participate.

Measuring performance is important to Kwik-Fit. The company's five million customers are encouraged to comment on the standards of service they receive. A free telephone helpline is available, and a reply paid questionnaire is given to every customer. Kwik-Fit's Customer Survey Unit also contacts more than 5,000 customers a day, within 72 hours of their visit to a Kwik-Fit centre. With this information, Kwik-Fit is able to identify ways in which it can further improve its services.

Today Kwik-Fit is the world's leading automotive parts repair and replacement specialist. As market leader, the Kwik-Fit brand is distinctive, well known, trusted and respected. The Group offers the best opportunities and support for all Kwik-Fit people, and aims to set world class standards in all that it does - which proves once again, 'You can't get better than a Kwik-Fit fitter'.

*Above left: Kwik-Fit fitters replacing an exhaust.*
*Above right: The jumping Kwik-Fit fitters featured in Kwik-Fit's famous advertising campaign.*
*Left: Sir Tom Farmer CBE, Chairman and Chief Executive established Kwik-Fit in 1971.*

# Merchiston Castle School – 'one of Scotland's finest'

Charles Chalmers first took pupils at home in 1828 from where he moved his growing numbers to Merchiston Castle in 1833. He was an innovative teacher at a time when teaching was restrictive and many schools in great need of reform. So successful were he and his successors that the school expanded to meet demand, as did Edinburgh itself as it engulfed Merchiston Castle's once rural setting.

In 1930 the 210 pupils were rehoused in Colinton House near Colinton village. The one hundred acres of grounds, closely bounded by the Water of Leith and the Pentland Hills, provide a peaceful setting both for academic study and for sports. The school is close enough to Edinburgh for regular outings which enhance a boy's education by introducing him to the arts and culture of the city. The surrounding countryside sets the scene for outdoor pursuits,

equally enjoyed by many pupils, which provide different challenges.

Merchiston Castle School celebrated its Centenary of 1933 in the company of the newly wed Duke and Duchess of York, later King and Queen. Half a century later their daughter, as Queen Elizabeth II, visited the school on the occasion of its one hundred and fiftieth anniversary. Her comments included praise for the boys' readiness to talk and their good manners. But then this is a Scottish school!

Scottish virtues of hard work, tempered by a sensible care structure for boys growing towards young manhood, are allied to traditional chalk and talk teaching methods to which proven and workable new ideas are added, to produce impressive results. Clubs and societies include chess, business,

*Below: The School and its rugby team in the late 1860s.*

ornithology plus a Young Farmers Club to add variety to a dozen team and individual sports. These range from athletics and cricket, via golf and tennis to rugby and shooting.

The unique Merchiston house system moves boys from house to house as they mature under the guidance of House Masters and teaching staff. Each house has its own ethos suitable to the working and non-academic needs of developing boys who can use quiet rooms, kitchenettes, games and hobbies rooms for their indoor spare time activities. Boys progress from small, companionable dormitories via open-plan cubicles to private study bedrooms which give pupils with greater responsibilities the space to organise.

### Ready, ay ready!

Boyish things, such as eating good food, camping and hiking, a Combined Cadet Force and responsible 'messing about in boats' are very much part of boarding school life here, both for boarders and for day pupils. The latter can be provided with accommodation after late evening events so parents need have no anxiety about their travelling home.

The school's fine musical tradition is enhanced by a choir of fifty, good enough to tour abroad and a Choral Society of a hundred. Orchestras and Jazz Bands are quite the norm in public schools but Merchiston has, in addition to these, a Close Harmony Group and a well turned out Pipe Band which is has proved as popular in France on recent tours as it is at home.

All boys proudly wear the kilt on Sundays and for formal events.

The Science Department may exist in a Georgian mansion but its pupils have recently added awards for Electronic Design, Engineering and Invention to the school's formidable University record of superior entrance numbers well matched by degrees.

School Expeditions to regions such as Kenya and The Canadian Rockies test adolescents' team work, organisational and personal capabilities in a hard environment. Merchiston balances this by providing opportunities for its young men to work together with girls from sister schools in producing plays and running social events.

The Church of Scotland Chaplain leads Merchiston's religious life of daily worship, spiritual education and counselling while Matron and her deputy, both nurses, care for the school's physical welfare. Behind the scenes are the administrative staff and those who clean and cater for the school, together with indispensable groundsmen and maintenance staff. Every member of the school's tight-knit community has an important and valued role to play.

Over the years Merchiston has added well designed and soundly equipped buildings to its stock in trade. The quality of the Headmaster and his Teaching Staff determine success in helping every boy to make the most of his talents and preparing Merchiston's pupils to take their place in a changing world.

*Above: The School today.*

# The Edinburgh Academy in the New Town

The elegant New Town symbolised the increasing wealth found amongst some of Scotland's burgeoning population. It was apparent that the comfortable middle classes of the New Town wanted their sons educated in the same environment. The old style of life where all classes lived hugger mugger in shared closes and tenements was fast going. The Royal Grammar School was neither in a fashionable location nor able to compete, in contemporary terms, in maintaining high Scottish educational standards. Following some years' consideration Henry Cockburn and Leonard Horner, later Warden of the new University of London, and John Russell, in 1824, established to meet these needs the pioneering Edinburgh Academy at the northern end of the New Town. Opened by Sir Walter Scott and led by Dr John Williams as first Rector, the school grew from strength to strength. Scottish schools, unlike the Classics-dominated English public schools, provided a broader subject-based curriculum than usual in the early Victorian era. Although many boys then walked to school from the New Town it became necessary to build boarding houses for those who travelled, by the developing railway system, 'frae a' airts' to the growing school. These distinctive buildings still provide term time homes for the boys and girls of the school community, some of whom fly in from abroad.

Dissatisfaction with the 'ad hoc' knockabout ball games played against the walls and buttresses of 'houses' and school rooms led to the bold decision to purchase the 'New Field' for use as a games field. Thus began the development through outdoor games of 'Muscular Christianity', team spirit, fair play and consideration for others by which the Empire was administered. The first international was played at Raeburn Place, now the home of the Edinburgh Academicals.

How very different things seem today. A new clientele of parents want an approach to education and to family life quite unknown to those of previous generations. And yet, the standards for work and behaviour demanded by caring families and teachers remain, in essence, unchanged.

*Above: The first Rector, Dr. John Williams.*
*Below: The 'Clacken', a game played here by the Ephors and Seventh in 1948.*

This, then, is the Edinburgh Academy's task. To maintain academic standards as a preparation for University and business-like careers at the same time as giving growing youngsters opportunities to develop as worthwhile individuals. For those intelligent children who, through illness, hearing problems, dyslexia and gaps in previous schooling, experience Specific learning difficulties the school runs a Learning Support Department, which also exists to assist pupils speaking English as a second language.

The happy Nursery caters for children between three and five who learn as much by constructive play as by the essential teaching which follows on this foundation. The Preparatory School at Inverleith takes youngsters through the magical world of learning by way of mastery of the delights of the elemental three Rs.

Here pupils are encouraged to build upon their individual rates of success by relating books and resources to the wonders of the world. The pleasant environment of school grounds next to the Edinburgh Arboretum is an idyllic location in which boys and girls gain confidence in themselves and their friends. Parents working to stern timings can rely on the After-School Care and Activities Service to fill their offspring's waiting times with a range of worthwhile and enjoyable activities. The eager enthusiasm of this age group is tapped by involvement in Arts and Games activities beyond the classroom including residential courses in Glen Doll. Transfers to the Senior School are carefully monitored so that there are no hiccups in personal or educational development.

The classroom is the base for Edinburgh Academy's academic excellence in all subjects. The well endowed art department caters for all levels of timetabled and free time endeavour in both visual and musical arts. Beyond the walls pupils can choose from the diversity of sports and outdoor pursuits, the latter afloat or in wild and beautiful country.

From the Fourth Form on all pupils participate in the Combined Cadet Force where volunteers may graduate to training new cadets.

Moral and careers guidance provide a steady foundation upon which to build the future. Academy pupils learn to accept responsibility for themselves and for the welfare and leadership of others in the community as they progress in their scholastic and social development.

*Top: The Academical Clacken and Ball race in 1949.*
*Above: A football match, Academy v Merchiston from 1949.*

# The story of Edinburgh's growing Dominion

Edinburgh's Dominion Cinema opened just over 60 years ago, and is today the only independent cinema on the East Coast of Scotland. Founded by Captain William Macpherson Cameron, and still run by the Cameron family today, the business was incorporated as Granada Cinemas (Edinburgh) Limited (no connection with the Granada chain) on 13 May 1937, and the Dominion Cinema opened its doors on 31 January 1938, showing the film Wee Willie Winky, starring Shirley Temple.

Captain William Macpherson had had a varied life prior to becoming a cinema owner. He had joined the Royal Scots as a teenager and had been sent to the front at the very outbreak of hostilities; he had risen to the rank of captain, and remained in the army until 1921. He then worked in the garage trade and the hotel industry before becoming involved in property building, and he set up his own building company, the Craighall Cast Stone Company. It was this company which was responsible for constructing the Dominion cinema; the frontage, which is today listed, is made of cast stone into which a pink pigment has been introduced. This caused something of a family row, as William's wife came from a family of masons, who strongly disapproved of William for having built a cast stone cinema.

*Below: Cinema 3 with 47 seats.*
*Right: Cinema 4.*

However, when William's labour force was called up for service in the second world war the Cast Stone Company's building yard was taken over by the Dunlop Rubber Company, who used it as a site for recycling rubber into tyres and gas masks, and the risk of further family disharmony was thus averted.

When the Dominion first opened it had a single auditorium with a seating capacity of 1360, and in those early days it ran 35mm film. During the war years, going to the cinema gave something more than just entertainment: it was a chance to relax and settle down for a few hours, watch the newsreels in the company of fellow patriots, knowing that every person in the audience shared the same hopes and fears, and then enjoy a good film - comfort, a boost

The most popular film ever screened at the Dominion in box-office terms was Braveheart, which, perhaps surprisingly, attracted much larger audiences at the time than more enduring classics such as Gone With The Wind and The Sound Of Music. The Dominion has always played an active role in the Edinburgh Film Festival and is an ideal venue for premières as it is a large cinema, with seating for 600. Recent premières include the Scottish première of Mrs Brown and the world première of the new film about Oscar Wilde.

With the customer always its top priority, the Dominion was the first independent cinema in Scotland to install the Hard of Hearing Loop system. Customers can also enjoy healthy snacks in the Dominion's cafe, which is open from 10am to 11pm.

The Dominion has grown since its early days, and a friendly team of some 48 staff now work there alongside the second and third generations of the Cameron family. William's son Derek took a keen interest in the cinema and in film generally from an early age, and helped out in various ways; sadly, William Macpherson Cameron died when his son was twelve, leaving his wife to run the cinema until 1953 when Derek took over. Derek is now Chairman, and the current joint Managing Directors are his sons Al and Michael Cameron, with daughter Lesley in charge of the Property Division.

The Cameron family has very successfully managed the Dominion Cinema in the Morningside area of Edinburgh for over 60 years, and has retained a loyal customer base by providing consistently high quality entertainment and an excellent service with the personal touch.

to morale, and entertainment too, and all for just a few shillings.

After the war, however, an increasing number of families acquired television sets and cinemas had to become more inventive to tempt their audiences away from their own living-rooms. The Dominion introduced a change of format in 1952 when it became the first cinema in town to have Cinemascope, and this featured heavily in its advertising of the day, promising the audience 'glorious technicolour' and 'wide screen', as a contrast to their own small monochrome screen at home. In 1972, the Dominion invested in twin auditoria to give cinemagoers a choice of film; in fact it was the first independent cinema in Scotland to convert to twin screens. A third auditorium was added in 1980, and a fourth in 1997; plans are now afoot for fifth and sixth cinemas, to give the audiences of the next millennium an even wider choice.

*Above: Cinema 2 with 331 seats.*
*Top: Cinema 1 with 574 seats.*

*A Ministry of Food Transportable Kitchen Unit at the Civil Defence emergency feeding demonstration, held at Springfield House, Edinburgh, in October 1953.*

# Acknowledgments

*Mrs Moira Alexander and Miss Elaine Smith at the Edinburgh Headquarters of the W.R.V.S; Jenner's Department Store, Prince's Street, and Edinburgh City Libraries for permission to reproduce the Jenner archive; Squadron Leader Bruce Blanche Ae\* BSc MSc DIC R Aux AF and the staff at the No. 2 Maritime Headquarters Unit, Royal Auxiliary Air Force, 25 Learmonth Terrace, Edinburgh; Mrs Helen Clarke at The People's Story Museum; Miss Helen Kane; Mrs Eileen Tait; Mrs Jean Smith; Dr Alan Thomson; Mr John Hutchinson of The Still Moving Picture Company; Mr Bill Brady and The Scotsman; Mr Nick Baldwin, Transport Archivist... and everyone else who played a part in the production of this book.*

*Thanks are also due to:*
*Peter Thomas who penned the editorial text,*
*Margaret Wakefield and Mike Kirke for their copywriting skills*